THE MAKING OF A CHOREOGRAPHER

De Valois at the height of her involvement with the repertory theater movement. Portrait by Vaughan and Freeman. The Dancing Times, *February 1930, frontispiece.*

THE MAKING OF A CHOREOGRAPHER

Ninette de Valois and *Bar aux Folies-Bergère*

Beth Genné

STUDIES IN DANCE HISTORY, NO. 12
SOCIETY OF DANCE HISTORY SCHOLARS
1996

ISSN 1043 7592
ISBN 0-9653519-1-2
Library of Congress Catalog Card Number 96-69521

To Mary Clarke *and* Selma Jeanne Cohen

Contents

Illustrations

"Will Be Valuable Someday": *Preface*

This book centers on Ninette de Valois's formative years as a choreographer and a shaper of British ballet, and on one of her works, *Bar aux Folies-Bergère*. Inspired by the celebrated Edouard Manet painting now in the collection of the Courtauld Institute Galleries, the work was commissioned by Marie Rambert for her company, then known as the Ballet Club, and premiered at London's Mercury Theatre in 1934. *Bar* is the only ballet that de Valois did for Rambert: it thus brought together, for the first and only time, the women who presided as matriarchs over the renaissance of English ballet in this century.

As a rule, de Valois saved very few of her choreographic notes. For *Bar*, however, a detailed score of the ballet's dramatic action and choreography miraculously survives in the form of a thirty-four-page notebook now in the Rambert Dance Company Archives. Discovered after Rambert's death in a cupboard in her home (along with a copy of her personally annotated score of *The Rite of Spring*), the manuscript had a note attached to the cover in which she had scrawled in her distinctive slanted handwriting—"will be valuable someday." Additional comments by Rambert, scattered throughout the score, increase this value, while offering a unique glimpse into the mind of de Valois's great colleague, admirer, and rival. The ballet's "script" (as Rambert called it), published here for the first time, is used as a springboard for a discussion of de Valois's working methods, personal notation system, and the cultural milieu of which *Bar* was a product.

Today, Ninette de Valois is better known as the visionary founder and longtime director of Britain's Royal Ballet than as a choreographer. However, the fact is that most of the ballets produced during the early years of the Vic-Wells company (as the troupe was known until about 1940, when the name was changed to Sadler's Wells) were hers, and she contributed regularly to its repertory until 1950. Her ballets were thus crucial to establishing company's identity. But they also brought in audiences and were viewed as important works by critics. Rambert, too, thought highly of de Valois as a choreographer: this is evident not only from the commission she offered her, but also from the comment she scrawled on the notebook. *Bar* remained in the repertory of Ballet Rambert until 1953 and was one of its most popular works.

In addition to Rambert and de Valois, *Bar aux Folies-Bergère* employed the talents of numerous other pioneers of twentieth-century British dance. The music was selected and arranged by Constant Lambert;

the scenario was by Ashley Dukes, Rambert's husband and the director of the Mercury Theatre; the stage manager was Antony Tudor. The original cast included Alicia Markova, Frederick Ashton, Mary Skeaping, Pearl Argyle, Diana Gould, Walter Gore, and William Chappell, who also designed the sets and costumes. Elisabeth Schooling, who inspired the ballet (although she only danced in it later), was another member of this pioneering generation.

Bar aux Folies-Bergère is exceptionally well documented visually. *The Sketch* ran full pages of photographs not only at the time of the premiere but also during the seasons that followed.[1] And there are a number of photographs taken in performance both at the Mercury Theatre and on the company's tours, with the original and later casts. Some of these action photographs give a vivid and immediate sense of the charismatic qualities of the early Rambert and Vic-Wells dancers.

The ballet is visually interesting for other reasons too. Chappell's designs, for instance, drew extensively on French art of the late nineteenth century, the period in which the ballet was set—not only Manet, whose painting inspired the work, but also Henri Toulouse-Lautrec. In the illustrations that follow, performance photographs are juxtaposed with their sources in paintings, allowing one to see how closely the designs reflected their visual sources and also in what ways they deviated from them. This use of painting as a choreographic and design source was modeled on the fusionist approach associated with Diaghilev's Ballets Russes. As we shall see, de Valois was deeply indebted to Diaghilev, as was Rambert. The second chapter examines the nature of this debt as well as de Valois's relationship with the Ballets Russes, the single most important experience of her formative years as an artist.

Another key experience was her involvement with the repertory theater movement. In the critical years of the late 1920s and early 1930s, when de Valois created her first mature works as a choreographer, she worked closely with three of the era's most innovative theatrical organizations—the Old Vic, the Festival Theatre, Cambridge, and the Abbey Theatre, Dublin. Her exposure to avant-garde stagecraft and "expressive" styles of movement continued her education as a modernist begun with the Ballets Russes. Her debt to the repertory theater movement and its influence on her "modern" choreography is discussed in the third and fourth chapters.

While not a major work, *Bar aux Folies-Bergère* is an interesting and representative example of British ballet in the decade following Diaghilev's death in 1929 and the dispersal of his company. During this period, British dancers and choreographers were forced back on their own, compelled to develop the resources at hand if their vision of creating a national dance company and audience were ever to be realized. The book opens with an examination of de Valois's early career, her experience with the Ballets Russes and its influence on her, her involvement with the repertory theater movement, and her first years as a choreographer. It then explores her relationship with William Butler Yeats and the Abbey Theatre, Lilian Baylis and the Old Vic, and Rambert's Ballet Club, an organization that had much in common with de Valois's company, but also differed from it dramatically. Finally, it turns to *Bar aux Folies-Bergère*—its genesis, its treatment of design, music, and choreography, its reception by critics. The volume concludes with the notebook that, with the prescience of a sibyl and the instincts of a pack rat, Rambert happily saved from oblivion.

Acknowledgments

I am deeply grateful to the many people who have helped make this book possible. First and foremost, I wish to thank Dame Ninette de Valois for generously sharing her recollections with me and for granting me permission to publish the notebook of her ballet *Bar aux Folies-Bergère*, which is reproduced in facsimile in these pages along with an accompanying transcription. The wit, humor, enthusiasm, and sharply analytical perspective she brought to our conversations together have been a continuing and vital source of inspiration for me. I am also deeply grateful to the Rambert Dance Company, in whose archives the notebook is preserved, for consenting to its publication, and to the company's archivist, Jane Pritchard, who supplied the necessary prints, read and commented on the manuscript, and was a fount of information about Marie Rambert, the Ballet Club, and British ballet in general.

I am also deeply grateful to Selma Jeanne Cohen for encouraging me to work in dance history, and to Mary Clarke, whose pathbreaking books on the Sadler's Wells and Rambert companies are indispensable for any study of twentieth-century British ballet. An early supporter of this project, she helped me in innumerable ways in my research on Dame Ninette. It is to these pioneering dance historians that this book is dedicated.

I also wish to express my profound thanks to Ivor Guest and to Ann Hutchinson Guest for their invaluable help from the earliest stages of the project, and my deep gratitude to those who allowed me to interview them about the ballet and their experiences in the de Valois and Rambert companies: the late William Chappell, Sally Gilmour, Maude Lloyd, Dame Alicia Markova, Pamela May, Lady Diana Gould Menuhin, Elisabeth Schooling, and the late Angus Morrison, who took off an entire day to help reconstruct the score of *Bar aux Folies-Bergère* and perform it on audiotape, as well as share his vivid memories of Constant Lambert. I am also indebted to the late Phyllis Bedells, whose recollections were so important in helping me reconstruct the dance world at the beginning of the twentieth century. I am very grateful as well to Kathrine Sorley Walker, whose beautifully detailed biography of de Valois (written with Dame Ninette) is the cornerstone of any de Valois research. I wish to express my gratitude to the staff of the following libraries and archives: Theatre Museum, London, Sarah Woodcock and Philip Dyer in particular; Royal

Opera House archives, Covent Garden, Francesca Franchi in particular; Royal Ballet School archives, Audrey Harman in particular; Royal Academy of Dancing library, Clement Crisp in particular; Dance Collection, New York Public Library for the Performing Arts, Susan Au in particular. Others to be greatly thanked are Richard Alston, Barbara Barker, Anna Blewchamp, Patricia Daly, Joan Erdman, Howard Friend, Liz Heasman, Stephanie Jordon, Vera Lyndall, Alastair Macaulay, P. W. Manchester, Sue Merrett, Selma Odom, Richard Ralph, David Vaughan, and the late G.B.L. Wilson. My colleagues at the University of Michigan have also been extremely helpful: Warren Hecht and Ken Mikolowski, who discussed Dame Ninette's poetry with me; Jessica Fogel, who read and commented on an early version of this manuscript; Susan Pratt Walton and Abigail J. Stewart, whose conversations with me about women's issues were consistently enlightening; William P. Malm and Joyce Rutherford Malm, who talked to me about Noh drama; Martin Walsh, who discussed Ernst Toller and German expressionist theater with me; and Roland John Wiley, whose studies of Russian ballet have been invaluable. Finally, I want to thank Joe Dowling, the former director of the Abbey Theatre and now the artistic director of the Guthrie Theater, Minneapolis, who found time in his busy schedule to talk to me about Yeats and the Abbey Theatre.

I am also extremely grateful to the Getty Grant Program. As a Getty postdoctoral fellow, I had the luxury of spending the better part of a year in England doing research in connection with this project. A University of Michigan faculty research grant helped support my work, my return research trips to England, and the costs of publishing Dame Ninette's manuscript. My deepest thanks as well to Lynn Garafola, who edited the manuscript with truly exemplary care, patience, and determination to see the job through, and whose knowledge of the Ballets Russes and its era made conversations with her on dance history a delight. Without this support, *The Making of a Choreographer: Ninette de Valois and "Bar aux Folies-Bergère"* would never have come to fruition.

Finally, and most of all, I would like to thank my husband, Allan Gibbard, and my family, Steve and George Gibbard, for their love and support. Allan talked with me about this project from the very beginning and read many a page; Steve set up the computer program on which I wrote the manuscript, and George was a helpful and sometimes hilarious critic. All of them helped me put things in perspective. —B.G.

EDITOR'S NOTE: In the 1920s and early 1930s, when the term "choreography" began to enter English dance parlance, the spelling of the word and its variants remained subject to fluctuation. In Ninette de Valois's published writings of the era, the "o" is usually omitted: hence, the title of her "Modern Choregraphy" articles published in *The Dancing Times* in 1933. These variant forms have been retained throughout the book when quoting from period sources.

THE MAKING OF A CHOREOGRAPHER

"Wonder Child" in the School of Hard Knocks: De Valois's Early Years

> When I look back on those wasted years between ten and fifteen I only feel a renewed anxiety to leave English dancers with some security and definite standards. Coming from an untheatrical background it was impossible for my mother to understand what I really needed to know and to whom to turn to for advice. In those days England had no Sadler's Wells, no Arts Council, no big private schools, and no institution such as the Royal Academy of Dancing devoting its work to raising the standard of teaching and giving advice and guidance throughout the country. The ballet was not recognized as a branch of the English Theatre; dancers were accepted as individuals on their individual merits and they had to search for their own teachers; how they arrived at their eventual state of execution was no one's concern.
>
> —Ninette de Valois, *Come Dance With Me*[1]

The woman who would do more than perhaps anyone else to change this state of affairs was born Edris Stannus on 6 June 1898 on her parents' estate, Baltiboys, near the village of Blessington in County Wicklow, Ireland, about twenty miles from Dublin.[2] Her family was mainly of Anglo-Irish heritage; her great-grandmother, Elizabeth Grant, was a Scot, the author of *Memoirs of a Highland Lady*. Her father was a career officer in the British army who fought in the Boer War and, having attained the rank of Lieutenant Colonel, was killed in action in World War I. Her mother, Lilith, was a cultured and talented woman, with an avid interest in the performing arts, and de Valois remembers playing the piano for the vocal recitals she sometimes gave at home.

De Valois's early childhood, as described in her 1957 autobiography *Come Dance With Me*, was happy and secure. She was the second of four children—three sisters and one boy. "Our lives," she wrote, "were very sheltered," ruled by nurses and governesses and bounded by the schoolroom. As a child, she was "intensely reserved and as obstinate as a mule—capable of 'the sulks' (as the nursery would say) brought to a fine art."[3] Her first and most powerful musical memory was of learning the steps of an Irish jig taught to her by one of the household servants that she performed with great gusto at parties. She remembers, too, being enthralled by a pantomime version of *The Sleeping Beauty* that she saw at the Gaiety Theatre in Dublin. And she remembers the intense pleasure of exploring the family's spacious nineteenth-century house—a "typical Irish country house," as she called it[4]—with its lawns, stables, woods, and gardens, and its fascinating kitchen world of "endless whitewashed rooms" that stretched the length of the house "below stairs."[5]

This idyllic childhood ended when de Valois was seven. Like many landed gentry of their era, the family found itself unable to maintain such a large property and had to move. Leaving Baltiboys was a traumatic event for the sensitive little girl:

> I was left standing midst the bustle of departure, at the window of our old nursery. My eyes looked on the lawns and paths of those gardens that I would play in no more....I did not cry, nor did I ask any questions as to when we might be coming back; I knew the truth and I wanted no comforting grown-up lies. There and then I deliberately tore my heart out and left it, as it were, on the nursery window-sill.[6]

De Valois was sent to live with her grandmother on the south coast of England in the small seaside town of Walmer, near Deal. There, like many girls of her age and background, she began lessons in what was then called "fancy dancing." Her first teacher, who came down from London every week, was the head assistant of Mrs. Wordsworth, a "well-known amateur teacher" whose "Edwardian School of Deportment," as de Valois called the establishment in *Come Dance With Me*, catered to girls of the better classes. The lessons, which were meant to instill etiquette as well as teach ballroom dancing, "answered," she wrote, "to a system known as Fancy Dancing; a quaint compromise of rudimentary steps such as the chassé and glissade combined with other steps fancy beyond belief."[7]

When her family moved to London, de Valois continued lessons with Mrs. Wordsworth herself, eventually becoming a "show pupil" and assistant. With Mrs. Wordsworth classes were more rigorous. In addition to social dancing, de Valois remembers being given "a certain amount of Dalcroze eurhythmics and they were well taught."[8] Accompanied by her mother, she also began to acquire a knowledge of professional dance in London. She saw—and was inspired by—Adeline Genée, Phyllis Bedells, Anna Pavlova, and Diaghilev's Ballets Russes. Her decision to forge a career in dance was greeted with horror by Mrs. Wordsworth, who had "a puritanical loathing of dance as a profession," viewing it as unsuitable for well-bred girls: "she would scrub floors," she told Mrs. Stannus, "before a daughter of hers went near the stage."[9] Mrs. Stannus, although worried about her daughter's education, "ragamuffin outlook on many things," and "independence,"[10] supported her ambitions and allowed her to train for the stage.

When de Valois was about twelve, she entered the Lila Field Academy, a professional theater school whose alumni included not only Phyllis Bedells but also Noel Coward. Here, the children "learnt something of everything," as de Valois wrote.[11] Early on, however, she was "set aside to specialize in the classical ballet section." In 1913, with a company of children from the school, she made her first tour, performing at music halls in London and at pier theaters in resort areas along the south coast:

> We were called The Wonder Children and presented an astonishing and

rather terrible programme of small ballets and short plays. I can also remember a precocious effort in the form of a revue—with the children depicting great stars.... I think I can boast of having danced on every old pier theatre in England! We worked very hard; I made ten solo appearances every night and received a salary of £4 a week. Out of this I kept myself, paid my term's tuition fees and saved. Lodging in those days cost about £1 per week.... We had no wardrobe mistress and no dressers. My mother had to buy my ten costumes and I had to take them with me in my own theatre hamper. I was responsible for packing and unpacking, mending, ironing, and all the necessary laundry work of these costumes and the care of my shoes and tights; this was coupled with eight performances per week and long Sunday journeys.... Miss Field was very strict, and our clothes and make-up had to be exactly as she ordained.[12]

Billed as the troupe's "prima ballerina," de Valois was "doomed," as she wrote, "to be Pavlova." Her speciality was an imitation of *The Dying Swan*, which she reproduced from notes made in the upper circle at the Palace Theatre, where the ballerina had danced the famous solo at her Wednesday matinees. Because of Pavlova's enormous popularity, it was not unusual for child performers to imitate her most famous dance. However, as noted by *The Dancing Times* editor P.J.S. Richardson, who caught the act in London in July 1914, the fifteen-year-old de Valois "render[ed] the episode... with great feeling, and fully deserved the applause that followed."[13]

A look at a typical "Wonder Children" program shows de Valois's

A class at the Lila Field Academy, 1914. De Valois is at the center of the group on the right, standing in front of the pillar. The Dancing Times, *December 1914, p. 95.*

HERE WE ARE!

(THE FIRST CHILDREN'S REVUE).

By LILA FIELD.

The Courier	Stephanie Anderson
The Belle of New York	Gwen Hope
American Beauties	Connie Wilde, Kitty Pounds,
and Eileen Dennis.	
Tickle (a Newsboy)	Joan Feist
The Sportsgirl..	Joan Batheuse
Philadelphia (A Ragtime Maid)	Merle Loftus
Bathing Girls	Dickie Pounds, Marjorie Mercer and
Lynda Tottenham	
A French Doll	Nonie Woodruff
Miss Ragtime	Molly Poulton
The Great Pavlova	Ninette de Valois
Cupid	Violet Kemplen

The Revue takes place in Miss Ragtime's Garden.

The following numbers are sung and danced in the order
as below.

Nobody	Joan Feist
Get out and get under	Joan Batheuse
You're my Baby ..	Stephanie Anderson and Nonie Woodruff
Cupid Dance	Violet Kemplen
When love creeps into your Heart	Joan Batheuse
Eastern Dance	Eileen Dennis
The Wedding Glide	American Beauties and Joan Feist
The Midnight Choo Choo	Gwen Hope
Popsy	Molly Poulton and Violet Kemplen
The Goblin Man	Dickie Pounds
The Swan Dance	Ninette de Valois
Je Sais que vous etes Jolie	Violet Kemplen
The Tango Girl	Molly Poulton
Imitations	Joan Feist
You made me love you	Gwen Hope
How do you do, Miss Ragtime ..	Molly Poulton

Costumes worn in the Russian Ballet designed and executed by Miss Cull,
"Playfrocks," 33, Moreton Street, Victoria, London, S.W.

General Manager - H. VAL KIMM

TIMES AND PRICES.

Orchestra Stalls, 2/6; Stalls, 1/6; Pit Stalls, 1/-; Pit, 6d.
Balcony Stalls: Reserved 2/-; Unreserved 1/- Balcony 6d.
The 2/0, 2/- and 1/6 seats may be booked at Pier Gates.
(Smoking allowed in Balcony only).
Matinees: Doors open 2.30. Evenings: Doors open 7.30.
All Tickets are sold subject to the right of the Management to make any alteration in
the Cast which may be rendered necessary by illness or other unavoidable causes.

*Program for Lila Field's "celebrated Wonder Children,"
West Pier, Brighton, week of 30 May 1914.*
Author's collection.

Swan Dance (as *The Dying Swan* was titled) placed among music hall turns like "The Midnight Choo Choo" and "How do you do, Miss Ragtime." The juxtaposition tells us a great deal about the position of ballet in England at the time. Apart from the Ballets Russes, which occupied a niche apart, neither ballet nor its practitioners were held in high esteem. In the hierarchy of serious art, ballet stood far below music, opera, or drama. Moreover, although visiting Russians such as Pavlova or Ballets Russes stars such as Vaslav Nijinsky and Tamara Karsavina might be lionized, their British counterparts lacked the status of other artists. In 1915, two years after de Valois began her performing career, the Empire, the last of the London variety theaters to present ballet as part of its regular program, disbanded its troupe. Henceforth, British classicists, including Phyllis Bedells, the Empire's first native-born première danseuse, would have to choose between finding refuge—under suitably Russified names —in the Diaghilev or Pavlova companies, or dancing, as de Valois would do throughout her early career, in revues, pantomimes, and other forms of commercial entertainment.[14]

In December 1914, de Valois climaxed her first years on the stage by auditioning for—and winning a place in—the annual Christmas pantomime at the Lyceum, a position she held until 1919. In the then small world of London dance, the post was an important one. Billed as the production's première danseuse, she led a corps of dancers in the "Grand Ballet" that traditionally ended the first half of the pantomime. It was one of the most popular parts of the evening, de Valois recalled,

greeted with thunders of applause from an audience that would have known no bounds to its indignation if such a spectacle had been omitted. The end of the scene always found one standing in a golden chariot, or reposing on a cloud, or lying in a seashell, for the tableau was always a manifestation of the "geographical" position of the pantomime; at that moment in time, it might be Dawn in a Garden of Flowers, Cloudland, or Under the Sea. The technique of the justly famed Transformation Scene never varied. A slow lifting of gauzes, a fading into scene after scene of fairylike splendour with miraculous lighting showing the splendours of the Lyceum's stage effects in that school of mechanical perfections belonging to the theatre of the Victorian era.[15]

When not reposing on a cloud or a seashell, de Valois *did* actually dance. Reviewing one of her performances in the pantomime *Jack and the Beanstalk*, P.J.S. Richardson offered a rare glimpse of the choreography and how the audience reacted to it:

> [Her] dance is a brilliant one, yet well within the power of the dancer. It includes an enchainement of petit batterie, some adage, and the very showy finish consists of a series of coupés, posés, attitudes en tournant, about a dozen fouettés, ronds-de-jambe en tournant, ending with the familiar déboulés. The dancer was loudly and deservedly applauded both during and at the end of her performance, and I honestly think that in her we have the future English première.[16]

At the Lyceum, de Valois "fell into the clutches," as she put it, of the ballet mistress Madame Rosa, who had been a prominent dancer in the Alhambra ballets of the 1880s. "Her feet were tiny and beautifully formed," de Valois wrote, "encased in very pointed, delicate shoes." "For me [however] her fascination lay in the fact that she had been partly trained by the great Italian ballerina of those Alhambra days—Palladina [sic]. I never tired of asking her about her lessons with the Italian."[17]

By this time, dismayed with the instruction offered at the Lila Field school and also, perhaps, in response to the rigorous training models described by Madame Rosa, de Valois had changed teachers. Her new mentor was Edouard Espinosa, who had created the *Jack and the Beanstalk* solo described by Richardson. A product of the French school, Espinosa had received his early training from his father, Léon, a noted danseur of the 1880s, who had studied at the Paris Opéra, danced in Paris and Russia, and been attached for a time to the Imperial Ballet. De Valois studied with Espinosa from 1914 to 1917. Like most English dancers trying to make a living in the theater, her lessons were short and sporadic. She saw Espinosa only three times a week for two half-hour private lessons and one general class. "[We] knew little or nothing of the slow state school training in other countries," de Valois wrote in 1977. As a result "too much was crammed into the half-hour sessions."[18] But the determined young dancer made the most of them. When the lesson was over, she would carefully write down everything she had learned. She then prepared her own syllabus, organizing the material into two coherent sets of exercises—or "courses of study," as she called them—that she practiced assiduously on alternate days for two hours at a time.

De Valois credits Espinosa with "saving" her feet, for at the Lila Field Academy she had been put on pointe without proper preparation. In fact, footwork was Espinosa's strength, and it may well be that her fondness for

A lesson with Edouard Espinosa, 1915. In the photograph to the right, de Valois (center) demonstrates développé à la seconde; below, she is shown in the third movement of a "simple" port de bras. The Dancing Times, *December 1915, pp. 96, 98.*

quick, precise footwork, which became a trademark of her choreography, had its origins in her training with him. "The lessons were very quick, with much *terre à terre* work. He excelled in the old French school of *petit batterie* and *pirouettes.*"[19]

Espinosa was a vigorous and outspoken advocate of good training who had a strong impact on the English dance community at a time when it badly needed him. With P.J.S. Richardson, he spearheaded the movement to reform and standardize dance training in Britain, an effort that led to the founding of the Association for Operatic Dancing (later the Royal Academy of Dancing) in 1920, an organization that, from its inception, de Valois herself enthusiastically supported.[20] She became one of Espinosa's star pupils, and he used her in various photographs, eventually published in *The Dancing Times*, to demonstrate correct technique.[21]

During the First World War, De Valois's schedule grew increasingly

De Valois demonstrating relevé. In the photographs accompanying his article "Some Errors in Tuition," Espinosa used de Valois to demonstrate (left) a "bad relevé front" ("the lifted knee [of the working leg] and the instep of the supporting leg are both in front, and this should not be") and (right) a correct one. The Dancing Times, *December 1916, p. 82.*

De Valois partnered by Felix Demery at the time she was studying with Espinosa. Photo by Hana Studios, Ltd. The Dancing Times, *December 1915, frontispiece.*

hectic. Her father, at first absent, then lost to her forever when he was killed in battle in 1917, could no longer help her financially. To support herself and pay for ballet lessons, she danced in music halls and appeared in West End musicals and revues, including *Laughing Eyes* (1919) and *Oh! Julie!* (1920).[22] Accompanied by a partner who was often a woman *en travesti*, she took her "operatic"—or classical—dance act on the rounds of the London and suburban music halls, playing the standard two shows a night, or three, when the act was booked at the Palladium. It was a hard life, and audiences were not always appreciative. "I knew the dread," she later recalled,

> of the provincial Monday night second-house audience: in those days it was an old music-hall tradition to give all turns a rough reception at that particular performance—it was never vindictive, but disturbing indeed would be the laughs, whistles and cat-calls that greeted every turn all over the country throughout the entertainment world on a Monday night second house.[23]

In addition to this grueling performance schedule, the young dancer began to take pupils herself. And as if this weren't enough, she spent the weekends during the war working in the kitchen of a military hospital in Park Lane. Later, she joined the staff of the Victoria Station soldiers' canteen, where she was eventually put in charge of a shift.

The appearances in music halls and West End musical shows produced a growing sense of disillusionment in the young dancer. A brief respite from the commercial theater came in 1919, when she was engaged as première danseuse for the first postwar "International Season of Grand Opera" at Covent Garden. But the uninspiring music and often hackneyed choreography of the commercial theater drained her physically and psychologically. In *Come Dance With Me*, de Valois writes of reaching a "dangerous state of boredom" in this period.[24] Possibly in an attempt to remedy this situation, she began to consider forming her own troupe and choreographing for it. By 1921, thanks to an engagement on a music hall circuit, the company was a reality. Headed by de Valois and her partner, Serge Morosoff, the ensemble included Margaret Craske, Vivienne Bennett, Audrey Carlyon, Vera Lyndall and four other women. For the half-hour program de Valois created four works, now lost. Jan Caryll, a New Zealand dancer who replaced Morosoff during the tour, recalled the presentation as being "ahead of its time": "the numbers," he wrote in his memoirs, "sat uncomfortably within a typical music hall bill."[25] De Valois, on the other hand, thought the program was "mildly successful," explaining that "the end of the venture after six weeks was mainly due to a very serious slump in the variety theatres."[26] However short-lived, the experience was a foretaste of things to come.

One of the few sources of inspiration for de Valois and the English dance public generally in these years was the Ballets Russes. She eagerly awaited the company's London visits, and in 1921, was among the small group of enthusiasts who attended numerous performances of *The Sleeping Princess* (as Diaghilev had renamed *The Sleeping Beauty*) at the Alhambra Theatre. This work was to have a profound influence on her vision of ballet.

By the time of *The Sleeping Princess*, de Valois had already had an opportunity to see the Diaghilev dancers at close range. In 1919, the great Italian pedagogue Enrico Cecchetti settled in London and accepted de Valois as one of his first English pupils. (She was introduced to him by Hilda Bewicke, an alumna of the Pavlova and Diaghilev companies, with whom de Valois had briefly studied.) It was the first time de Valois had taken a daily class. Her fellow students included Marie Rambert, Ursula Moreton, Margaret Craske, and, occasionally, Lydia Lopokova, all of whom would figure importantly in her life to come. From Cecchetti, de Valois later wrote, she "learn[ed] the meaning of symmetry, the hidden beauty of the studied detail, the harmony that can be achieved in movement and the meaning of *ports de bras*."[27]

Unity of movement was a fetish with him; I have seen him hurl both abuse and his stick at a dancer who attempted to learn a step by executing it only from the waist down. He would always prefer first to be given the proof by his pupil of some knowledge pertaining to the head and body movements...thus we were expected to master the épaulement first, even to the point of sometimes marking the step with our hands.... He had no respect for a technician with little else to offer outside his technical feats; as a great exponent of the Italian School of precision and virtuosity this attitude made him unique.[28]

Young as she was, de Valois had a selective eye and her own distinctive opinions. She did not accept the Maestro's teachings indiscriminately. Although he left a "great imprint on the English School,"[29] she felt that his "special system...possibly cramped his full powers. He had many sound theories that will live for ever as a part of all ballet teaching, and he had other theories that are already discarded."[30]

For de Valois, Cecchetti was above all a teacher who worked best with the young professional as opposed to the pupil in training. His talent, as she saw it, was to refine talent rather than develop it from scratch:

> Cecchetti never produced a ballerina solely trained under his method. This was a criticism levelled at his teachings by many great dancers, and I would say that the comment is not an unfair one. He undoubtedly had a genius for giving a dancer a certain stamp and finish; he also had (through certain aspects of his special system) a great capacity for correcting a serious fault.[31]

Cecchetti's other great strength, in her view, lay in teaching young choreographers. Her first serious efforts as a choreographer coincided with her years of study with him, and it may well have been the inspiration of his classes that impelled her to think with increasing seriousness about creating her own dances. In his classes, she learned important lessons that deepened her understanding of Diaghilev's choreographers, especially Léonide Massine:

> [Cecchetti] was very much the artist-teacher as opposed to the pedagogue.... I would say that I have always felt that he was an ideal professor for young choreographers to study with, and by far the best teacher for the artists of the Diaghilev period of the 1920s. Massine was a devoted pupil, and undoubtedly in the end his choreography was more understandable and easier to execute for those who had studied with Maestro Cecchetti.[32]

Cecchetti's close connection with the Diaghilev company allowed de Valois to mingle with dancers she had previously admired from afar, while they, in turn, came to know her personally. Massine, who would be an important influence on her own choreography, was among those who now entered her world. Another was Lydia Lopokova. During the respite in Ballets Russes activity that followed the failure of *The Sleeping*

Princess, the two stars organized a small troupe, which they invited de Valois to join. The Russians prepared their new venture with zeal, and the result proved a revelation to de Valois, accustomed as she was to the hackwork of the music hall. "The choreography was of an order undreamt of in any of my previous experiences," she recalled, "and the disciplined routine of class and lengthy rehearsals in preparation for the opening filled me with a sudden feeling of dedication that was an entirely new sensation."[33]

In 1923, Cecchetti left London, and "for a few inspiring months" de Valois studied with Nicolas Legat. His teaching emphasized rather different qualities than the precision and virtuosity so important to Cecchetti. As she later wrote:

> I was soon made aware of expansion in my movements and experienced a new form of a more fluid strength enter my body.... He was, above all, a teacher who gave you a sense of existing in your own right, and never as an automaton for him.... I certainly found with him a path that extended my work, and I became more attentive to the importance of a more expansive expression in my classroom movements—valuable tuition for me.[34]

Her classes with Legat ended in the fall of 1923, when, at the recommendation of the Russians who had seen her in class and in performance, she was invited to join Diaghilev's Ballets Russes.

Diaghilev's impact on the twenty-five-year-old dancer was crucial. He cultivated her taste and expanded her horizons; even today, she sees him as the single most important influence on her ideas for the development of British national ballet. In the Ballets Russes, de Valois was given the example of a serious repertory company that far surpassed any existing ensemble. She acquired a first-hand knowledge of the company's dancers and choreographers, and through them, a knowledge of the Imperial Ballet School in St. Petersburg. As a member of the corps and, later, as a soloist, she danced in works by Fokine, Massine, Nijinsky, Nijinska, and Balanchine, as well as in truncated versions of *Swan Lake* and *The Sleeping Princess*, thus becoming intimately acquainted not only with some of the most innovative and important choreographic developments of her own day, but also with those of the immediately preceding decades. For de Valois, this exposure to the Ballets Russes was a turning point in her life.

When de Valois left the Ballets Russes in 1925, she had already formulated in her mind the goal of establishing a native British ballet company and affiliated school that would eventually find a place among the great state-supported dance organizations of Russia, France, and Denmark. By doing this, she hoped to create an institution that would elevate the art of dance, as created and performed by rigorously trained British artists, to what she believed to be its rightful status—an art on a par with music, opera, and drama, and recognized as such by her compatriots.

The idea of creating a British national company was not new; it had been in the air through most of the previous decade when de Valois was coming to maturity as a dancer. As early as 1916, both Richardson and Espinosa had agitated for the development of such a company, and Phyllis Bedells had led the fight for English dancers to be treated as equals of their Russian colleagues by refusing to adopt a Russian name.[35] Espinosa, in fact, had briefly put together a group intended to be the nucleus of a future British ballet company, an effort that came to nought after a single performance. And in the 1920s, Marie Rambert began developing the small group of dancers that became the Ballet Club and, eventually, Ballet Rambert.

But more than anyone else, it was De Valois who turned the talk into action and the dreams into reality. She took the first modest step toward her goal in 1926, when she founded "The Academy of Choregraphic Art" to train the personnel for such a company. In the summer of that year she approached Lilian Baylis, the director of the Old Vic Theatre, with a carefully worked out scheme for the formation and development of a repertory ballet company attached to the "Old Vic," which then alternated performances of Shakespeare and other plays with opera. Baylis was impressed by de Valois's clear-sighted and pragmatic plans as well as by her determination. However, she could only offer part-time work—coaching actors in stage movement, arranging dances for Shakespeare plays, and presenting small dance performances as "curtain raisers" before operas. De Valois was disappointed, but treated the offer as an opportunity, and so, on 13 December 1928, as part of the Old Vic's Christmas show, the curtain rose on her ballet *Les Petits Riens*. Danced by the pupils of her school, the work was followed by Engelbert Humperdinck's opera *Hansel and Gretel*.

These little productions proved so successful that in 1931 a small company was established to give regular ballet evenings under the aegis of the Old Vic. At first, these performances alternated between the Old Vic and the Sadler's Wells Theatre: hence the company's first name, the Vic-Wells Ballet. In 1932, however, the company moved to the newly opened Sadler's Wells Theatre. Here, it quickly grew, acquiring a large and loyal audience and an extensive repertory of classical and modern ballets.

To support herself during this period, de Valois continued to dance in revues, most notably Charles B. Cochran's 1927 *White Birds*, in which she appeared as an apache and choreographed the "Traffic in Souls" ballet for Anton Dolin. On occasion, she also returned to the Diaghilev company for guest appearances. In 1926, de Valois became the choreographic director of the Festival Theatre in Cambridge, a post she held until 1931. Among the admirers of her work was the Irish poet William Butler Yeats, who persuaded his young compatriot to return to Ireland and work with him at the Abbey Theatre in Dublin. Beginning in 1927, she made regular trips to the Abbey, where she organized a ballet school, staged a number of his Plays for Dancers and performed in them, and created several short ballets on Irish themes suitable for young dancers.

Between 1930 and 1933, de Valois also participated in a theater group that was to have a profound impact on the development of British ballet—the Camargo Society. Founded in 1930 by P.J.S. Richardson and Arnold Haskell (in part to fill the void created by Diaghilev's death in 1929), it produced a series of performances by British dancers and choreographers that demonstrated to the public that ballet was not the exclusive preserve of the Russians. De Valois, who was a founding member of the society, helped devise its organizational plan, and, along with Marie Rambert, provided the dancers who appeared in its productions. De Valois also contributed several ballets to the Camargo repertory, including *Danse Sacrée et Danse Profane* (1930), *Cephalus and Procris* (1931), *La Création du Monde* (1931), *The Jackdaw and the Pigeons* (1931), *Fête Polonaise* (1931), *The Origin of Design* (1932), and one of her most important and enduring works, *Job* (1931).

By 1933, when the Camargo Society went out of existence, de Valois's own company was flourishing. Not only had it grown in numbers, but it had found a permanent home at Sadler's Wells, where it was offering ballet programs on a regular basis. The following year, in order to devote herself full time to the company, she ended her seven-year association with the Abbey Theatre. For the remainder of the 1930s—indeed, for the rest of her working life—the company, its repertory, dancers, choreographers, and affiliated school commanded the whole of her attention. She was determined to create a stable and self-perpetuating organization that would provide British dancers with the security of a living wage and a congenial atmosphere for the optimal development and display of their talents. A woman of vision and indomitable will, she lived to see the fulfillment of her dream. Today's Royal Ballet is fully the equal of the state-supported institutions that had once been her inspiration.

From the beginning de Valois planned not only for the present but also for the future. With the example of the Ballets Russes before her, she set about creating an institution that could survive "many a director," including herself.[36] Such continuity, she realized, depended not only upon the existence of a permanent performing ensemble, but also upon the existence of an affiliated school—a "nursery" or "laboratory" where future dancers and choreographers could be systematically trained and an identifiable "house" style developed. She viewed school and company as parts of a continuous cycle, with company members drawn from the ranks of the school and older artists returning to its studios as teachers.

From the beginning, too, de Valois had to perform a multitude of widely diverse and difficult roles. No detail was too small for her attention. She became an administrator of genius, managing, on a minuscule budget and with an initial corps of only six female dancers, not only the day-to-day running of the company but also that of the school. She planned programs, conducted rehearsals, and looked after the books. In addition, she developed a syllabus for the training of her dancers that ensured them artistry as well as a strong technique, and she served as a strict but also inspiring teacher. This training would lead to the distinctive style that brought the company international acclaim, while also producing top-notch dancers. Foremost among them was Margot Fonteyn, whose talent de Valois had early sensed and, then, carefully and assiduously developed.

Drawing on her experience with the Diaghilev company, de Valois believed that it was not enough to develop new dancers: new choreographers were needed, along with a repertory that was both modern and British to create a "native" company style. In the 1920s she herself served as the company's "choregraphist" (as she was identified in the programs), although, in acknowledgment perhaps of her artistic limitations, she appointed Frederick Ashton as its resident choreographer in 1935—an inspired choice, as no one did more to foster the British style of dance. As a choreographer, Ashton had been "discovered" and nurtured by Marie Rambert. Rambert remembers de Valois coming backstage after a performance of Ashton's first ballet, *A Tragedy of Fashion*, full of enthusiasm and telling her that she (Rambert) had found a "real choreographer."[37] But though Rambert may have discovered Ashton, it was de Valois who gave him the security of a regular wage, placed her confidence in him for the long term and, most importantly, provided the "laboratory" of dancers for him to work out his ideas.

An ardent propagandist for the cause of British ballet, de Valois used her skills as a charismatic public speaker and persuasive writer to promote the cause of dance. She lectured to organizations throughout the country and published important articles on British ballet in *The Dancing Times*. In her 1937 book, *Invitation to the Ballet*, she lucidly and forcefully presented her assessment of dance in Britain and Europe generally, outlined her own vision of ballet as a theater art form, and argued for the development of a national British company. Well aware of the importance of audience development, she became the president of the London Ballet Circle, which been formed to educate the growing public for British ballet.

De Valois was not only the artistic director of the Vic-Wells company, but also one of its performers. By necessity, she danced a wide variety of parts, but she particularly excelled at demi-caractère roles (such as the eccentric tightrope walker in her 1932 comic ballet *Douanes*) that made use of her precise footwork, strong attack, and spirited, forceful personality. Early Vic-Wells patrons remember with special affection her bright, cheeky Swanilda in *Coppélia*, while in the brusque, no-nonsense housemaid of *A Wedding Bouquet* Ashton immortalized aspects of her off-stage personality.

Finally, in these early years, de Valois was a choreographer. It was her job to provide the Vic-Wells company with most of its early repertory, and she did this with works that not only appealed to audiences, but also kept them coming back. But before examining this aspect of her career, let us first turn to the years she spent in the Diaghilev company and its influence on her ideas about choreography, modernism, and technique.

"Everything of Value":
De Valois and Diaghilev

> The writer can say that everything of value to do with the presentation of ballet, the study of choreography and the development of the artist, that she has ever learned, came from this apprenticeship in the most famous of companies; a company whose existence for some twenty-five years was the fruit of the mind and will-power of one individual.
>
> —Ninette de Valois, *Invitation to the Ballet*[1]

This sweeping statement, made by Ninette de Valois in her book *Invitation to the Ballet*, refers to the Ballets Russes and its director Serge Diaghilev. Although de Valois spent only two years with the Diaghilev company, its impact was powerful enough to become, in her words, the "main influence" on her career.[2] The statement is not an isolated one, nor is it merely a courteous bow to a great man. The power and extent of Diaghilev's influence on de Valois is a theme that runs throughout her writings from the 1930s to the present day.

De Valois joined the Ballets Russes in September 1923 and remained with it until August 1925. In the next three years she made "three or four returns to the company...for short periods" as a guest artist.[3] Although she had already achieved some prominence in London as a dancer, she joined the company as a member of the corps de ballet. She did not audition for the position, but was engaged on the recommendation of company members who had taken classes with her at Cecchetti's London studio and danced with her in the small company formed by Massine in the spring of 1922. Cecchetti, whom Diaghilev also consulted about the appointment, gave his approval as well.[4]

Working with the Massine troupe had rekindled her enthusiasm for dance, but dance as it was performed by her Russian colleagues. The Russians, as de Valois put it, had "ruined" her for the pantomimes and revues that had been her lot.[5] "I joined the Russian ballet," she wrote, "to escape none too soon from the commercial theatre, which, after twelve years, had led to a *cul de sac* of listlessness and disillusionment."[6] The Diaghilev troupe was her entrée into a new world of dance.

When de Valois joined the Ballets Russes in 1923, the company was well into its second and final decade of existence. Its heroic years were past; the famous seasons dominated by Nijinsky, Bakst, and Fokine belonged to a world that had vanished with the war. Massine, too, had left the company, although he returned in 1925 to mount *Zéphyr et Flore*, in which de Valois danced. The failure of *The Sleeping Princess* had shaken

Diaghilev's confidence and undermined his hopes for a classical revival. Still, the Ballets Russes remained a thoroughly going concern. There was a regular touring season, a home base of sorts in Monte Carlo, and a new creative center in Bronislava Nijinska, Diaghilev's resident choreographer from 1921 to 1925. In 1925, Balanchine joined the choreographic roster and created his first works for the company. Of the company's dancers at this time, de Valois wrote:

> It was an age of youth in the ballet—this was emphasized by Vera Nem-chinova's appointment as the classical ballerina. The maturer members with established reputations as first dancers in their respective spheres of execution were [Lubov] Tchernicheva, [Felia] Doubrovska, [Lydia] Sokolova, [Ludmila] Schollar, [Anatole] Wilzak, [Stanislas] Idzikowsky, [Leon] Woizikowsky, [Thadée] Slavinsky, [Nicolas] Kremneff, and [Nicolas] Zvereff. The younger newcomers consisted of [Alice] Nikitina and myself, [Anton] Dolin, [Serge] Lifar, and [Constantin] Tcherkas. [Alexandra] Danilova, [Tamara] Gevergeeva, and [Alicia] Markova did not join for another year.[7]

As a member of the corps de ballet, de Valois danced in nearly every work in the large and varied repertory. She appeared in Fokine's *Narcisse*, *Daphnis and Chloe*, *Petrouchka*, *Papillons*, *Carnaval*, *Les Sylphides*, *Cléopâtre*, *The Polovtsian Dances*, *Schéhérezade*, and *Thamar*; Massine's *Midnight Sun*, *The Rite of Spring*, *The Good-Humoured Ladies*, *Contes Russes*, *La Boutique Fantasque*, *Le Tricorne*, *Cimarosiana*, and *Zéphyr et Flore*; and in Nijinsky's *L'Après-midi d'un Faune*. She also danced in a two-act version of *Swan Lake* and in *Aurora's Wedding*, which Nijinska had patched together from the Prologue and third act of *The Sleeping Princess*.

All these ballets left a mark on her later career, but none proved as influential on her thinking as *Aurora's Wedding*. The work brought her into close contact with Nijinska, and a vision of ballet in which the classical past and the modernist future seemed to meet. Nijinska coached the younger woman in the pizzicato of the ballet's "Florestan" pas de trois and worked with her on the role of Red Riding Hood. She also taught de Valois her own "infinitely more interesting choreographic development of the famous 'finger variation'—danced in the prologue by one of the fairies. I had the honour to be taught this personally by Nijinska when I took her place in this dance, in an effort made to release her from some of her dancing roles."[8]

Nijinska was to be de Valois's last great teacher.[9] Her influence on the young dancer was profound:

> Madame Nijinska was my first experience in the Russian School of a choreographer-teacher, and she proved to be a very great influence on my future outlook. I studied the Russian School in these specialized circum-

stances for eighteen months, and then Nijinska left us; but she left one inspired young artiste behind whose whole outlook was now beginning to take a very different view of choreography and the ballet.[10].

Even in the classroom Nijinska remained a choreographer. As a teacher, she covered

the same basic work [as Legat], but developed and extended beyond its conventional source, because her choreographic ideals and tendencies were to be interwoven into our daily class.... I was lucky to have [had] the Legat experience first, it was as if I had studied the alphabet of a language carefully before I moved forward to a complex form of writing evolved from it. Madame's classes were interesting but difficult. Again I found them strengthening and in no time I noticed an improvement in my elevation. With her I had, as my second experience with the Russian School, a choreographer-teacher opening up my mind and strengthening my body. She was obsessed with correct breathing and gradually one saw the important relationship between breathing and movement. Correct breathing soon became a habit, so much so that it is now difficult to recall the theory involved that she would expound at great length. She taught us a very definite approach to body movement, as intricate as any contemporary dance, but strictly in relation to the classical school.... I was... enjoying this new

Bronislava Nijinska (center) conducting a rehearsal of the Ballets Russes in London, 1924. Alice Nikitina and Anton Dolin are on the extreme left.
Private collection, New York.

approach to a class, and realised that it was all closely related to the ballets that we had to execute for her. I was young and looking for new ways of thinking, and I had already begun to feel a deep interest in choreography as opposed to mere execution.[11]

Of all Nijinska's ballets, none made so powerful and enduring impression on de Valois as *Les Noces*. It was one of the first works she learned after joining the Ballets Russes, and, even today, three-quarters of a century later, she remembers it as a shocking, exciting, and profoundly impressive introduction to the world of modern ballet, one that she never forgot:

> Time and again I have written and spoken of the effect of Nijinska's *Les Noces* on me. The strange and powerful score of Stravinsky's—mystical, ritualistic, the soul of Russia, was both felt and realised by all the dancers concerned. We became just dedicated parts of the whole—to dance in it was to forget the audience, for it required tremendous concentration, and that added to the exhilaration of the experience. It was always the same, no number of performances ever dimmed its musical and choreographic freshness, its challenge to one and all.[12]

In her years with the Ballets Russes, de Valois danced in nearly all of Nijinska's ballets for Diaghilev—*Les Biches*, *Les Fâcheux*, *Les Tentations de la Bergère*, and *Le Train Bleu*, in addition to *Les Noces*. Clearly Nijinska admired her talents. She may have even have seen aspects of herself reflected in the young, strong-willed dancer, with her quick, powerful footwork, forceful attack, and all consuming curiosity about every aspect of dancemaking. It was on de Valois that Nijinska worked out her own role in *Les Biches*—the pearl-draped, cigarette-smoking Hostess, who presides over the interesting assortment of guests at an ultra-1920s house party. During rehearsals, and with the encouragement of Diaghilev, his personal assistant Boris Kochno, and the ballet's composer, Francis Poulenc, the astonished de Valois was "plucked...from the corps de ballet."[13]

In addition to this extensive repertory, de Valois also danced in the operas produced by Diaghilev in Monte Carlo in 1923–1924—Chabrier's *L'Education manquée*, Gounod's *Le Médecin malgré lui*, *Philémon et Baucis*, and *La Colombe*—as well as in the many operas, including *Carmen*, *Roméo et Juliette*, and *Manon*, produced by the Monte Carlo Opera with the participation of the Ballets Russes. These opera-ballets were important in that they provided de Valois with the opportunity to work not only with Nijinska but also with the young Balanchine: both "were responsible," as she later wrote, "for the choreography of a fairly stiff onslaught of opera ballets."[14] Nijinska arranged the vision solo for her in *Thaïs*, and she remembers Nijinska's work in *La Nuit sur le Mont Chauve* and Balanchine's in *Herodias* as "ballets of outstanding merit produced in the restricted medium of opera."[15] Another delight was Balanchine's "deft and apt" choreography for Ravel's opera *L'Enfant et les Sortilèges*, which received its premiere in Monte Carlo in 1925.[16]

From the beginning, de Valois had sensed the exceptional talent of the young Russian who replaced Nijinska in 1925, for she had participated in his audition as a choreographer for Diaghilev. Her recollection seems to be the only eyewitness account of this momentous occasion, which took place during Diaghilev's winter season in London in 1924:

> One Sunday morning I was summoned to Astafieva's studio with about six other artists. Balanchine was there, young and anxious-looking. He had an engaging charm and a great sense of humour which had made him popular with us, although he had only been with the company for about ten days. His dancing had proved to be rather less than indifferent, but we suspected in him some other form of distinctive talent. For two solid hours we learnt a choreographic conception of his, set to a Funeral March…(I never hear this music without calling to mind that Sunday morning). I worked with a will, for I was as acutely aware as others of his gifts. Just about midday Diaghilev, Kochno and [Serge] Grigorieff arrived, and we went through our choreographic patterns. On such occasions Diaghilev was an enigma. Face impassive, manner aloof; we were all robots, from Balanchine downwards, and there was no means of fathoming the impression made on our director.[17]

Balanchine's choreography, like Nijinska's, left a deep impression on de Valois:

> How refreshing was his originality! I can remember taking part in many small duets and ensembles arranged by him in the various operas; he charged these dreary experiences with a new life and interest, and no demands on him could curb his imaginative facility. His great musical sense never failed to make the most of the material offered to him, even when confronted with that outlet so universally dreaded by all choreographers—the opera-ballet.[18]

A pas de trois that Balanchine arranged for de Valois, Alexandra Danilova, and Felia Doubrovska during the Monte Carlo opera season that followed his acceptance into the company confirmed the nature of Balanchine's "distinctive" talent. De Valois no longer remembers the name of the opera for which the dance was created, but the brilliance of Balanchine's choreography remains clear and bright after three-quarters of a century. The choreography left her "swooning in the dressing room and solemnly assuring everyone that he was a 'genius.'"[19]

After two years with the Ballets Russes, de Valois returned to London. Although she had been steadily advancing within the Diaghilev company, she had decided to abandon her career with the Russians to work toward the goal of establishing an English national company.

But could or would de Valois have been able to conceive of such an institution without the example of Diaghilev? At the time of the formation of Vic-Wells there was virtually no "high art" tradition on which to build. As we saw in tracing her early career, ballet in early twentieth-century England was largely confined to the music hall and variety stage: it was viewed as popular entertainment rather than a serious art form. To be sure, Adeline Genée, the Danish-born ballerina who reigned at the Empire Theatre from 1897 to 1907, had a devoted following of ballet lovers, as did Phyllis Bedells, her English pupil and successor. But however loyal or even knowledgeable, this following had little in common with the society audience of Covent Garden or the cultivated public attracted to the Ballets Russes, especially before the war. Moreover, even in its heyday, the Empire was never entirely free of associations of sexual impropriety: indeed, its spacious promenade and bars were well-known hunting grounds for London's better class of prostitutes. This ambiance inevitably left a mark on the ballet offerings that were the theater's chief attraction. In a 1935 article about Diaghilev's influence in England, Tamara Karsavina pointed out that English attitudes toward ballet in the early years of the century retained a good dose of Victorianism: "The Victorian opinion considered ballet only as a delight to the eye, and not exactly a righteous eye at that. The moral opprobrium had worn itself out by our times, but no credit was given to the ballet in England as to a dignified and deep art capable of stirring the noblest human emotions."[20]

The Ballets Russes modified such attitudes by offering the example of serious repertory ensemble that was the equal in intent and execution of existing theater and opera companies. De Valois put it this way:

> The discovery of "*Ballet Russe*" could be likened to landing on an outer space planet, and finding microscopic life in every crevice. Gone for good was the self-conscious dainty understatement; gone the plump lady disguised as a male partner; gone the distorted relics of early romanticism, the tinkly tunes of the old ballet scores—those obliging efforts written to satisfy the ballet master and more often the ballerina. The orchestra pit took over, fortified by the works of distinguished composers who were aware of their rights and demanded a proper hearing. Gone also, with a resounding landslide, were the efficient but complacent stage-sets for state operas and ballets, and in stepped the great painters of the era.[21]

The Ballets Russes provided both the stimulus and the model for de Valois's native English troupe. In proposing to Lilian Baylis that a ballet troupe be formed and placed in the company of "serious" music and theater, de Valois was merely following in Diaghilev's footsteps.

In the Ballets Russes, de Valois first encountered large numbers of dancers trained at a single, stable institution devoted entirely to the development of the dancer. Graduates of the Imperial Ballet School in St. Petersburg, they had passed through a carefully graded system that prepared them in every way for life on the stage. From childhood, they had worked in the atmosphere of the theater, dancing the mazurka in *Paquita*, the Garland Waltz in *The Sleeping Beauty*, and the many other numbers that Petipa included in his ballets for children. Upon completion of the eight-year course of study, they entered the corps de ballet, advanced through the ranks of coryphé, demi-soloist, and soloist, before graduating (if they were talented enough) to principal roles.

In addition to providing a strong technical foundation, the Imperial Ballet instilled in its dancers a self-disciplined approach to their art. This de Valois particularly admired:

> One of the most impressive things about the Russian Ballet was the methodical outlook of state-trained dancers. They had two masters to serve—the ballet and themselves. The nine months season would be devoted to the study and mastering of the *rôles* required of them by the theatre, the daily class a means of obtaining the necessary physical discipline. But towards the end of the season, and for at least three-quarters of the ensuing three months' holiday, all concentrated on strenuous classroom studies under other professors than those appointed by the director.[22]

Although far from home and the institution that had trained them, Diaghilev's dancers acknowledged their schooling and reaffirmed their loyalty to it with every daily class.

The systematic training and rigorous standards of the Russian dancers stood in marked contrast to de Valois's haphazard early training. As we have seen, she shuttled from teacher to teacher, and job to job, and her lessons were both irregular and sporadic. "When I look back on those wasted years between ten and fifteen," she later wrote,

> I only feel a renewed anxiety to leave English dancers with some security and definite standards. Coming from an untheatrical background it was impossible for my mother to understand what I really needed and to know whom to turn to for advice. In those days England had no Sadler's Wells, no Arts Council, no big private schools, and no institution such as the Royal Academy of Dancing devoting its work to raising the standard of teaching and giving advice and guidance throughout the country.[23]

In 1926, when de Valois opened her Academy of Choregraphic Art, conditions for training English dancers had not appreciably changed. In an article published in *The Dancing Times* in 1933, she deplored the "lack of opportunity" that allowed "very few of our dancers [to] know what it is to develop their powers in a really congenial atmosphere."[24]

To create this "congenial atmosphere" for English dancers, de Valois took the Imperial Ballet School and company as a model. From the beginning, a school was attached to the Vic-Wells company. Initially, the curriculum included only dance and theater courses. However, when it became financially possible, general education subjects were added. By 1951, the school was recognized by the Ministry of Education as a full primary and secondary school, and in 1955, like its Russian model, the junior school, at least, became a residential institution. In the early years, however, the school and company existed under one roof, an arrangement that allowed de Valois to combine teaching and managerial responsibilities, and to keep an eye on the talent emerging from the school. As was the case at the Imperial Ballet School, students were brought up in the atmosphere of the theater, imbued with a devotion to their art, and inculcated with the high standards that were ever before them in the form of principal dancers. The interaction of students, performers, and teachers fostered the creation of a company style and allowed the dancer to develop within the framework of a received tradition. As de Valois later wrote, "My experience with the Diaghilev company in the 1920s had shown me that here was a group of people brought up in a great tradition in their own country.... I wanted a tradition and I set out to establish one."[25]

De Valois recognized, then, that the strength of the Ballets Russes stemmed not only from the innovations of its choreographers, but also from the traditions of the Imperial Ballet. "Diaghilev," she wrote, "had the advantage of the resources that had emerged from the Imperial Ballet.... For years he...had behind him a great root from which could spring his ideas and their development."[26]

The early Vic-Wells repertory attests to her determination to acquire the "classics" as soon as possible. By this, she meant the major French and Russian works of the nineteenth century. By 1934, only three years after the initiation of regular company performances, the repertory included full-length productions of *Swan Lake*, *The Nutcracker*, and *Giselle*, and Acts I and II of *Coppélia*.[27] By 1939, when *The Sleeping Beauty* premiered, the Vic-Wells Ballet had acquired virtually all the nineteenth-century repertory existing at that time in the West outside Denmark—a remarkable achievement for a company of its size, youth, and limited finances.[28]

A factor in the decision to mount these works was the presence of ballerina Alicia Markova on the Vic-Wells roster. Hired by de Valois in 1933, Markova had the strong technique, exceptional lightness, and refined artistry needed for roles such as Giselle and Odette/Odile. Even more important, however, was de Valois's firm belief in the importance of a classical foundation for the company as a whole. Her commitment to this foundation was stated as early as 1926 in "The Future of the Ballet," an article published in *The Dancing Times*. "As a complete theatrical art," she wrote, "there is no question that the teachings of the classic school are the sure and only foundation—limitless in its adaptability it consequently proves its power to meet the varied requirements of the theatre."[29] In a later article she elaborated: "Every well run company needs a policy, however mobile, and here we are confronted with the question of some stabilising basis establishing the company's own 'tradition'.... [T]he Sadler's Wells Ballet might be said to have based its structure on a close study of the old classical ballets."[30]

Given Diaghilev's reputation as an innovator rather than a traditionalist and his company's limited nineteenth-century repertory, attributing de Valois's interest in "the classics" to them may well seem odd. Yet it was through the Ballets Russes that she gleaned most of her information about nineteenth-century ballet in general, and Petipa's works in particular. De Valois's first introduction to a full-length Petipa ballet was Diaghilev's production of *The Sleeping Princess* in 1921.[31] At the time de Valois was studying with Cecchetti, and the many Diaghilev dancers she met at his studio may have further stimulated her interest in the production and its problems. In any case, de Valois had the opportunity to observe the ballet over a relatively prolonged period and to see a number of ballerinas—Olga Spessivtzeva, Vera Trefilova, Lubov Egorova, Lydia Lopokova, Vera Nemchinova—in the role of Aurora.

Looking back from the vantage point of the 1950s, de Valois stressed the importance of the ballet in awakening the interest of the English public in the "classics":

> In retrospect, I regard the failure of the Diaghilev *Sleeping Beauty* as of secondary importance when compared with the interest that it aroused in traditional classical ballet: it could be said that the seed of true appreciation had been sown in a minority of the slow-but-sure British public, but it was a minority that remained steadfast and faithful to this new aspect of the ballet.[32]

Given that *The Sleeping Beauty* eventually became her company's signature piece, the long-term importance of the Diaghilev production cannot be underestimated. Drawing on her memories of the ballet and her own experience in dancing the one-act version that Diaghilev cobbled together from the original, de Valois realized that *Beauty* was an ideal vehicle to exploit and develop the talents of her company, including the ballerina who succeeded Markova, Margot Fonteyn. As de Valois wrote in *Step by Step*: "It was fortunate for our future that England was the one country to have seen his version in its first full-length presentation; this influence has had far-reaching effects on the English scene and the result has been commented on time and again outside the country."[33]

Diaghilev was also responsible for introducing de Valois to *Swan Lake*. Her initial reaction to the two-act version staged in 1923 for the former Maryinsky ballerina Vera Trefilova was largely negative. She found the production dull and old-fashioned, and the poor level of the corps work disappointed her. What "saved" the work for her was Trefilova's luminous dancing, which became one of the most powerful and important memories of her Diaghilev days:

> My most sharply outlined recollection is the revival of *Le Lac des Cygnes* at Monte Carlo, with Madame Vera Trefilova as guest artist. The work of the *corps de ballet* was painstakingly revived by those members of the Company who had been with the Imperial Ballet. I found myself uninterested; the ballet and the music struck me as old-fashioned and boring. It took Trefilova to save me from complete disillusionment: here I sensed the greatness of the execution and the perfection of the central structure of the ballet.

The Fairies in the Ballets Russes production of The Sleeping Princess, *1921. From left: Bronislava Nijinska, Lubov Egorova, Lydia Lopokova, Felia Doubrovska, Vera Nemchinova, and Lubov Tchernicheva. Photo by Stage Photo Company. The Dancing Times, December 1921, p. 29.*

In a way I was not altogether to blame; in my raw state it was difficult to develop a sense of proportion at a time when the relationship between the modern and the classical ballet was less close than it is today. In the staging of a modern production, I was used to the highest contemporary standards in dancing, décor, costumes, and music; alongside this state of perfection, I was confronted with a very indifferent and abbreviated classical revival; by our standards of today the *corps de ballet* had not the highest classical efficiency of dancing that is found in modern companies. The Diaghilev Ballet of my time was mainly a group of first dancers and soloists; the actual *corps* was very uneven, and not well balanced as a whole.

It took time for me to understand the influence of the classical tradition on the Company's work; enlightenment did not come until after I had left, and I had found time to reflect on the whole experience.[34]

However "indifferent and abbreviated" the Diaghilev *Swan Lake* may have been, it remained the fullest version of the ballet that de Valois would see until her own company mounted its complete version in 1934. To be sure, in 1932 the Camargo Society had produced the ballet's second act, with Olga Spessivtzeva as Odette, and also presented the full-length

Giselle, in which the ballerina gave her powerful—and justly celebrated—interpretation of the title role. De Valois served as ballet mistress for these productions and also danced in them, as did the members of her company: they were thus the immediate forerunners of her own productions. Although she may have seen Pavlova's version of *Giselle* (which the ballerina presented in London in 1925 and 1930) and various snippets from *Coppélia*,[35] it was Diaghilev's "classics"—*The Sleeping Princess, Aurora's Wedding*, and the two-act *Swan Lake*—that comprised pretty much the sum of de Valois's experience with the traditional repertory at the time she set about recreating it for the Vic-Wells company.

The Ballets Russes not only exposed de Valois to the classical repertory, but also introduced her to the personnel needed to stage it. In 1932, with the help of Lydia Lopokova, she contacted Nicholas Sergeyev, the former chief régisseur of the Imperial Ballet who had mounted *The Sleeping Princess* for Diaghilev as well as the *Giselle* staged at the Paris Opéra in 1924 and both the *Giselle* and *Swan Lake* produced by the Camargo Society in 1932. De Valois offered Sergeyev a ten-year contract to produce *Coppélia, Swan Lake, Giselle*, and *The Nutcracker*, for Vic-Wells: later, *The Sleeping Beauty* was added to the list.[36] Sergeyev had brought to the West "notation books that contained the Petipa ballets in full, as they were originally notated by Stephanoff [sic],"[37] a reference to the rehearsal scores and choreographic notations dating from the 1890s and early 1900s in the system devised by Vladimir Stepanov and refined by Alexander Gorsky.[38] In the Vic-Wells production of *Swan Lake* every effort was made to be faithful to the Maryinsky "original." For example, the traditional mime scenes that Diaghilev had abandoned were now restored:

> The second act of the *Lac de Cygnes*, as played by the Diaghilev ballet and the latter-day companies, includes (in lieu of the old mime scene at the opening between the Princess and Prince), an arrangement of dance movements. Until Nicholas Sergueff…came to London to mount *Lac des Cygnes* in its entirety on the Vic-Wells Company of English dancers, the London ballet lover was ignorant of the existence and the significance of this mime scene. This…company still makes a point of retaining this original form….The scene is particularly lovely, difficult to play, and an excellent test traditionally for the young dancer of this generation; it is, moreover, an important link between the ballet of to-day and yesterday, and that, in itself, is sufficient reason why it should be left to fulfil its mission.[39]

In *Beauty*, too, fidelity to the Maryinsky version was the young company's goal. Sergeyev reinstated the original finger variation in place of the version choreographed by Nijinska that de Valois had learned and performed in *Aurora's Wedding*.[40] These are two small examples, but they clearly reveal her intent and the stress she laid on the accurate reproduction of the original. Her commitment to authenticity extended to the musical score as well. Sergeyev, whom she describes as "unmusical to a degree bordering on eccentricity," would sometimes "pencil out a bar of music, which, for some reason, wearied him." The offending bars would be restored by Constant Lambert during the lunch break, and a small choreographic movement added to cover the musical director's "tracks."[41]

Sometimes, however, considerations other than accuracy determined her approach. The various dances from *The Nutcracker* that Diaghilev had insisted on interpolating in *The Sleeping Princess* were dropped from the Vic-Wells production not because they were inauthentic, but because the company already had *The Nutcracker* in its repertory.[42] Certain interpolations remained, however. Indeed, it was not until many years later that "The Three Ivans," the rousing character number choreographed by Nijinska to the coda of the Wedding pas de deux in *The Sleeping Princess*, was finally dropped from the Royal Ballet's production of *Beauty*.[43] Moreover, over the years, various sections of the ballet, including the Garland Waltz and Aurora's variation in the Vision Scene, were rechoreographed by Frederick Ashton and Kenneth MacMillan.

The strength of de Valois's commitment to the traditional repertory, even in the face of her limited experience with it, suggests that the force of tradition in the Diaghilev company was more powerful than outward appearances would indicate. If this traditionalism was not expressed in the Ballets Russes repertory, it was revealed in the attitude of the dancers, their teachers, and Diaghilev himself, and in what de Valois once described as "the entire atmosphere of the Imperial Ballet removed to France."[44] From her colleagues, she must have heard a great deal about the Maryinsky repertory and the importance of the bits and pieces of it kept alive by the Ballets Russes. "Progressive as Diaghilev was, he was a great traditionalist at heart," she has said.[45] Judging from her passionate response to the "classics" encountered in his company, the Ballets Russes was a potent—if largely unacknowledged—force in the transmission of the Russian classical tradition.

✳ ✳ ✳

Like Diaghilev, de Valois did not view modern choreography as an isolated entity, but rather as part of an integrated whole embracing music, design, and dance. The final work was meant to be a synthesis of art forms in which each of the elements played an equally important part. In England, this fusionist approach was typically seen as a Diaghilev innovation and singled out by critics as one of the most attractive features of Ballets Russes productions—and their most important "lesson." An unsigned article (most probably by the editor, P.J.S. Richardson) with the suggestive title "What Diaghileff Has Taught Us" summed up this lesson in 1919 for readers of *The Dancing Times*:

> A ballet is not confined to the product of the work of the teacher or choreographer. It is a synthesis of the sister arts of dancing, music and painting, and these must be so artistically blended as to form one homoge-

nous whole. The Russians have made "thoroughness" their watchword, and they have taught us the amount of importance that attaches itself to the music and décor.[46]

De Valois learned first hand what such unity entailed just before the opening of Massine's ballet *Zéphyr et Flore*, in which she danced one of the Muses:

> One day in the rehearsal room we had a dress parade of the costumes. Diaghileff and [Georges] Braque, the designer, were both present. The nine muses were very depressed, our costumes seemed dull and incomplete, and Diaghileff, overhearing our grumblings, told us to "stop wondering whether the costumes suited us, but to consider instead whether we suited the costumes." He went on to tell us that the costumes had been designed to fit the ballet and the scene and not, as we had imagined, for each individual dancer. The next morning I went to the theatre to see the backcloth for the ballet. It was then that I understood. In this simple cloth lay the key to everything that one could not find an explanation for in the costumes. My mind could put them together there and then, and I stood as entranced as if the whole ballet had been paraded for my special benefit.[47]

In her five-part series, "Modern Choregraphy," published in *The Dancing Times* in 1933, de Valois stressed the need for the choreographer to be knowledgeable about and closely involved in all aspects of production. Thus, her school offered not only ballet classes but also courses in set and costume design (taught by Vladimir and Elizabeth Polunin, scene painters for Diaghilev); it also boasted a music library, a reading library, and a theater art section.[48] When staging her major ballets of the 1930s—*Job* (1931), *The Rake's Progress* (1935), and *Checkmate* (1937)—as well as *Bar aux Folies-Bergère*, de Valois worked closely with the composer (or arranger) and designer to create a stylistically unified whole. In almost every way, these works aspired to the collaborative ideal she had learned from Diaghilev.

De Valois in Les Fâcheux. *Reproduced from* Théâtre Serge de Diaghilew: Les Fâcheux *(Paris: Editions des Quatre Chemins, 1924).*

By the 1960s, the idea of ballet as a synthesis of art forms had ceased to be the credo of the former Sadler's Wells company, something that today de Valois regrets.[49] Frederick Ashton, for instance, tended in his later years to rely on arrangements of preexisting music—Chopin in *A Month in the Country*, Rachmaninoff in *Rhapsody*—as opposed to scores written for the work at hand. More typical of his earlier period—and Vic-Wells ballets in general—was *A Wedding Bouquet* (1937), which had a libretto by Gertrude Stein and music and designs by Lord Berners. This is not to say that original music and original designs were always a feature of early Vic-Wells productions, any more than they were of Diaghilev's. Indeed, both Ashton and de Valois choreographed a number of ballets to music written for other purposes. However, the model, first gleaned in Diaghilev's works, always remained her goal, a key to her vision of modern ballet as an integrated, innovative art form.

Diaghilev's influence was also evident in the one-act format that de Valois identified with modern ballet. She described the "completely self-contained, one-act ballet" as *the* "modern format," and saw Diaghilev as its father:

> Creatively speaking, in the theatre, the English school has followed the modern conception of ballet (again a heritage of Diaghilev) in the form of emphasis on the completely self-contained one-act ballet.
>
> This form, in its purest conception, was born about forty years ago; at that time it was welcomed as an effort to re-establish the greater principles of choreography, including that of its relationship to the better forms of music; the timely birth of this new order spelt the death knell of the numerous elongated, decadent, and musically insignificant ballets of the late nineteenth century. We are left today only with the few surviving masterpieces of that time. The highly concentrated one-act ballet did much to embellish and widen choreography—particularly in the sphere of modern experimental work. It is the basis of the English theatre school; although we have familiarised ourselves with the handful of the great classics that have survived the last century, we are still unfamiliar with the basic handling of full-length ballet in creative work.[50]

A "modern" three-act ballet did not enter the Sadler's Wells repertory until Ashton's *Cinderella* in 1948, while the first full-length "all-British" production had to wait until 1957, when John Cranko choreographed *The Prince of the Pagodas*, which had music by Benjamin Britten, sets by John Piper, and costumes by Desmond Heeley. The company's precarious finances surely influenced this predilection for shorter works. Money was not the only factor, however: already in the 1930s the company had expended considerable sums on mounting full-length versions of nearly a half-dozen classics. Rather, both Ashton and de Valois viewed the one-act format as a vehicle for "creative" modern expression in ballet.

Following the model of Diaghilev, de Valois made the development of young talent—especially British talent—one of her key concerns. During the 1930s she commissioned music from Gavin Gordon, Geoffrey Toye, and Constant Lambert, and designs from William Chappell, Hugh Stevenson, Rex Whistler, Sophie Fedorovitch, Cecil Beaton, and Vanessa Bell. Bell was the only member of this group who was primarily an easel painter. In this, de Valois differed markedly from Diaghilev, who commissioned the vast majority of his designs from easel painters. Chappell, moreover, was a designer who also doubled as a dancer.

De Valois's two greatest "finds" were Frederick Ashton and Margot Fonteyn. Although it was Marie Rambert who initially discovered Ashton, it was de Valois who offered him the stability of a large-scale organization to practice his art. From the beginning, de Valois realized that a resident choreographer was essential to her enterprise to give it a creative center. What Massine, Nijinska, and Balanchine had been to the Ballets Russes in the 1920s, Ashton and de Valois herself became to Vic-Wells in the 1930s. Fonteyn, on the other hand, was not only a protégée of hers but also her "discovery." De Valois spotted Fonteyn's singular talents early on and, like Diaghilev with respect to Nijinsky, cultivated them assiduously, providing the proper atmosphere for their development and encouraging Ashton to exploit them in his ballets.

The first decade of Vic-Wells, then, witnessed the emergence of a major English dancer and a major English choreographer, along with the production of forty-one ballets. Like Diaghilev, de Valois was committed to the development of new repertory, although whether she played as active a role as Diaghilev in shaping this repertory is unclear. Like Diaghilev she sought out and fostered new talent. But, except for her own works, there is no evidence that she continued to have much creative input once new ballets had been commissioned, whereas Diaghilev retained a hand in all phases of production, demanding, on occasion, major alterations in the score, sets designs, and costumes.

Diaghilev left de Valois not only a rich legacy of ideas, but also the personnel to help implement them. The disbanding of the Ballets Russes after his death in 1929 added to the pool of émigré dancers on whose resources and experience she drew throughout the 1930s. Nicholas Sergeyev, who staged her productions of the classical repertory, has already been mentioned. So, too, has Lydia Lopokova, the former Diaghilev star whom de Valois has described as her "greatest friend in the theatre."[51] Not only did Lopokova conduct the preliminary negotiations with Sergeyev that culminated in his ten-year Vic-Wells contract, she also calmed his outbursts in the studio with a "vigorous flow of Russian," as de Valois put it, that "would make him see sense."[52] Lopokova appeared in some of the earliest performances of the company, and in 1933 danced the role of Swanilda in *Coppélia*. Most importantly, she and her husband, the economist John Maynard Keynes, "took on themselves," as de Valois wrote, "the care of the British Ballet." Their home on Gordon Square in the heart of Bloomsbury was "for me and for other dancers a refuge from everyday life.... The Camargo Committees... met at this house and I went there for advice in all my troubles. Young impecunious artists were given many splendid luncheons and suppers there."[53] It was Keynes, moreover, who arranged for the Camargo Society to give its final two performances at Covent Garden for delegates of the International Postwar Conference of Economists, thus raising the money to discharge the Society's debts and allow it to dissolve. As a result, the Vic-Wells company received—free of charge—the sets, costumes, and scores for several ballets, including de Valois's *Job*. The Camargo Society also gave its cash in hand to the Vic-Well's Ballet and, in 1936, made possible the company's production of Ashton's *Apparitions*—a princely gift.

Diaghilev also presided over the early development of the Vic-Wells's first major ballerina, Alicia Markova. English by birth (her real name was Lilian Alicia Marks), Markova received her early training in the London studio of Serafima Astafieva, a former dancer with the Ballets Russes. In 1924, when Markova joined the company, she was only fourteen. De Valois took her under her wing, and they remained close until she left the company in 1925. Late in 1931, after a Ballet Club performance in which Markova had danced, de Valois told her "that 'it was about time' that I appeared with her Vic-Wells Ballet."[54] Markova made her debut with the company in January 1932, and from 1933 to 1935 (when she left to form her own company with Anton Dolin) she was its prima ballerina. Her personal reputation attracted a sizable audience to the "Wells," a good part of which remained even after her departure. The company, in turn, served her well, mounting the full-length productions of *Giselle* and *Swan Lake* that sealed her triumph as a ballerina. By 1935, as P.W. Manchester later wrote,

> Her work was done and she could go no further by staying there....She had stayed long enough to secure the future of English Ballet, but there was no real place in it for her. Only by birth was she an English dancer, and whatever the development of our Ballet she must have remained always a brilliant anachronism. For that reason she was not an easy dancer to fit with rôles in the native repertoire that the Wells was building. On the last night, Miss Baylis patted Markova's hand while she blandly told us that "they couldn't afford to keep her any longer". But whatever the reason for her going, the Vic-Wells was ready to stand on its own feet.[55]

There was one crucial aspect of the Vic-Wells company that was untouched by the Ballets Russes—administration. Although de Valois was the founder, artistic director, and guiding spirit, the company was never a one-woman operation. Her goal was the creation of a stable, ongoing institution that could function independently of her, as opposed to an organization like the Ballets Russes, whose survival depended on the singular nature of Diaghilev's personality and genius. She fervently believed that if the company did "not survive many a 'Director,' it will have failed utterly in the eyes of the first dancer to hold that post."[56]

In her determination to create as stable an institution as possible, de Valois worked from the start to make the company, if not financially profitable, at least self-sustaining. By ultimately linking it with the state, she further increased its chances for long-term stability. Although Diaghilev's arrangement with the Monte Carlo Opera guaranteed the Ballets Russes a modicum of support during the 1920s, it was his ability to coax support from wealthy, if unpredictable patrons that allowed the company to weather the vagaries of the marketplace. He did nothing, however, to guarantee the survival of the Ballets Russes beyond his death, and once he was gone, the company collapsed. Its winter residency notwithstanding, the Ballets Russes was basically a touring company, with a debilitating performance schedule that took its toll on the dancers. Indeed, one of the reasons de Valois left the company was the "domestic disorder"—the exhausting round of classes, rehearsals, and performances, minimal pay, and less than respectful treatment from the management that was the lot of most of the dancers. These were conditions that de Valois sought to ameliorate. Indeed, her deep concern for the physical and mental well-being of her dancers enabled her to write by the 1950s:

> I do not think that the life we led would be very popular among repertory ballet artists of today. By comparison it was certainly very much harder, and I doubt whether, if ballet had been in the strong position that it is today, Diaghilev could have kept his company together, except with a greatly changed order of things on the domestic front.[57]

Diaghilev left a deep imprint on virtually every aspect of the company that would become the Royal Ballet. On de Valois herself his influence was well-nigh incalculable. He rekindled her love for dance at a time when thankless jobs on the commercial stage were causing it to ebb. He offered her the model of a company that treated dance as a serious art form, the first such model that she had ever encountered. He revealed the classical traditions that lay beneath the modernism of the Ballets Russes and introduced her to the dancers and teachers who could pass them on. Finally, through his productions of Nijinska, Massine, and Balanchine, he taught her the importance of a modern repertory to the growth of a creative organization.

De Valois has never ceased to acknowledge her debt to Diaghilev. She is as proud of it today as when she opened her first school seventy years ago. In 1987, she told the following story:

> A much treasured remark was made to me by Vera Nemchinova, who was a famous Russian Ballet ballerina of the 1920s. Many years had passed, then we met again after the Royal Ballet's triumphant opening at the old Metropolitan Opera House in New York in 1949. "Diaghilev gave us all something," she said, "but you took something from him." If I did, I took it when exulting in the many minor appearances that I made in his ballets, and in seeing the whole great machine at work day after day.[58]

"The Future of the Ballet":
De Valois and Modern Choreography

De Valois had been creating dances for herself practically since childhood. She provided some of the choreography for her early recital programs, the Lila Field performances, and her opera ballet appearances, and all the choreography for her short-lived touring group in 1921. These early efforts are lost now, but from their titles and the fragmentary evidence of reviews it seems likely that they were modeled on the divertissements offered by Anna Pavlova and her company and by Phyllis Bedells and Adeline Genée—a repertory of short classical and demi-caractère dances. A typical program for her touring troupe included a Hungarian dance by Brahms, Johann Strauss's "Blue Danube Waltz," Grieg's Albumblatt no. 7, and works by the less well-known composers Theodore Lack and Dorothy Foster.

A photograph of the dancers in flowing Greek-style dress also suggests the influence of the freer forms and plastique associated with Isadora Duncan and the Greek revival movement. In the case of de Valois, this influence probably originated with Mrs. Wordsworth, who taught a form of "Greek" dancing in which the students—wearing floor-length approximations of ancient dress—took poses modeled on classical art and performed line and chain dances.[1] Greek dancing, both in this amateur form and the more technically grounded systems developed by Ruby Ginner and Margaret Morris, was considered "far more respectable than ballet dancing," as Gweneth Lloyd has said, by people of de Valois's background and class.[2] Wordsworth extolled "the perfect harmony of...movements of arms, hands, body and feet," and her "Greek" dances were meant to develop health and grace in her pupils, while sharpening their artistic sensibilities.[3] With her loathing of the stage, she "regarded it the duty of anyone under her tuition to eschew the theatrical profession at all costs."[4]

What transformed de Valois's approach to choreography was her experience with the Ballets Russes. In the three years she spent as a member of the company, she danced in seminal works by the masters of twentieth-century ballet. She participated in the creation of works by Nijinska, Massine, and Balanchine. And she danced in shortened versions of *Swan Lake* and *The Sleeping Beauty*, works that embodied the Russian classical tradition. Among the founders of twentieth-century ballet companies, only Balanchine could lay claim to a similar body of experience.

In essence, de Valois treated her Diaghilev experience as an apprenticeship—a time for watching, absorbing, learning. It was never her intention to make a long-term career with the impresario. Indeed, she quickly real-

De Valois as a Bacchante in Narcisse, *1920s. Photo by Vaughan and Freeman.* The Dancing Times, *February 1926, p. 591.*

ized that life with the Ballets Russes—with its debilitating tours, payless paydays, and exiles "engulfed," as she wrote, "in a whirlwind that was not of their seeking"[5]—held no future for her. Rather, as with her previous teachers, she used the experience to grow. Thanks to her years with the Ballets Russes, she gained firsthand knowledge of its organizational structure and a deep appreciation of its repertory. No less important, she could say that she had danced with this most illustrious of companies.

De Valois left the Diaghilev company in February 1926. Five months later, she published an article in *The Dancing Times* on the "future of the ballet." In its own way, this essay was no less a manifesto than Fokine's 1914 letter to *The Times* summarizing his vision of the "new ballet." Accompanying the article was a striking photograph of the dancer "as she appeared in the Diaghileff Ballet." Wearing a tunic slit to the thigh, she is plunged in a luxurious backbend; her feet are bare, her head thrown back, her hair loose and streaming. Nothing could be further from the genteel, upright classicist who appears in earlier issues of the magazine. On the page opposite the unlaced bacchante was an announcement for the school that was meant to carry her vision of the future forward. It had a rather grand and unusual name: The Academy of Choregraphic Art. Although ballet—or "operatic dancing," as it was usually called—was the basis of the curriculum, de Valois eschewed the term for a neologism that was only beginning to enter English dance parlance. In the new and striking name for her school, de Valois implied that something more than "operatic dancing" would be taught there, and in her article she explained why.[6]

At issue, she stated, was "the contest between the classical ballet of the eighties and the modern choreographical studies."[7] This "much-discussed subject" she now proceeded to address, not only to provide a vision of the future (which, in her view, lay with the moderns), but also to plead with the "anti-moderns...if not for their co-operation, at least for their enquiry into a matter which they are viewing through smoked glasses."[8] Into a climate of polemics and dissent, she brought reconciliation and a vision that was clear, logical, and historically broad.

In the course of the article de Valois assessed the new ideas that had invigorated the London dance community when she was growing up. She wrote approvingly of "the Hellenic School with Isadora Duncan as its figure head [that] has shown the emotional powers that lie hidden in the theory of broader and freer body movement." She noted, too, the great and salutary influence of the "plastic school on the classic," adding that "the result has been most satisfactory."[9]

However, the "true theorists" of "modern choreographical studies," the only "choreographists" whose "creative works… can be considered seriously" were the dancemakers associated with Diaghilev. She named them in the order of their appearance on the dance scene—Fokine, Nijinsky, Massine, and Nijinska. "Nijinsky," she mourned, "has been lost to the world of art through ill-health—but we still have the remaining three and they are the only three that can be looked to at the moment for clear theoretical explanation."[10] De Valois did not explain what this meant, but implied that anyone who studied in her new "academy" would find out.

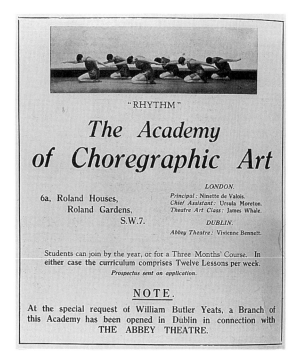

"RHYTHM"

The Academy of Choregraphic Art

6a, Roland Houses,
Roland Gardens,
S.W.7.

LONDON.
Principal: Ninette de Valois.
Chief Assistant: Ursula Moreton.
Theatre Art Class: James Whale.

DUBLIN.
Abbey Theatre: Vivienne Bennett.

Students can join by the year, or for a Three Months' Course. In either case the curriculum comprises Twelve Lessons per week. *Prospectus sent on application.*

NOTE.

At the special request of William Butler Yeats, a Branch of this Academy has been opened in Dublin in connection with THE ABBEY THEATRE.

Advertisement for the Academy of Choregraphic Art with a scene from Rhythm. The Dancing Times, *January 1928, p. 590.*

For de Valois the difference between Diaghilev's choreographers and the Greek revivalists was less a matter of originality than schooling. Indeed, Nijinska's work, to say nothing of her brother's, was as "radical" and "modern" as anything Duncan and the Greek revival people had done (and set to music that, in many cases, was far more "revolutionary"). However, Duncan's limited technical preparation and undeveloped training methods left her ill equipped to explore the full resources of human movement and build an enduring foundation for her art. As far as de Valois and the choreographers of the Ballets Russes were concerned, "the teachings of the classic school are the sure and only foundation—limitless in its adaptability it consequently proves its power to meet the varied requirements of the theatre."[11]

The key phrase here is "limitless in its adaptability." For de Valois the most vital forms of contemporary dance had evolved from the resources of the *danse d'école*, enriched by outside influences (like the "Hellenic" school) that allowed it to break new paths, from the barefoot "naturalism" of Fokine's Duncan-inspired choreography and the spasmodic expressionism of Nijinsky's *Rite of Spring* to the neoclassicism of Nijinska's stabbing pointework in *Les Noces*. For de Valois, "ballet" was a term encompassing a wide range of movement, even as she insisted that the choreographer of a ballet no less than its performer had to bring to the work a solid background in the *danse d'école*. It was this, she believed, that best prepared the body to meet the demands of even the toughest choreographer, that gave it flexibility, control, strength, and endurance, as well as the latitude in leg movement that came with the development of turnout.[12]

The modern movement, de Valois insisted, "was not the outcome of a whim or drastic revolution," nor, she added, did "expansion...spell expulsion [or] construction, destruction." "No art ever comes to a standstill. The theatre, accompanied by drama, painting and music, progresses steadily through experiment and research."[13] To illustrate her point, de Valois urged a comparison of dance with the evolution of music and the other arts, quoting the music critic Ernest Newman on the evolution of musical styles: "'As with the vocabulary of art, so with its forms. Broadly speaking each of these has grown so imperceptibly out of its predecessors that no ordinary intelligent musical mind that could think in terms of the earlier form could find any difficulty in adapting itself to the later.'"[14]

Thus, like the composer and musician, playwright and actor, the choreographer and dancer needed a thorough knowledge of the historical repertory of forms on which a particular tradition is founded and from which it continues to grow. Hence, de Valois stressed the analogy of dance with the other arts: just as the actor had to be able to play Shakespeare as well as Shaw, and the musician Mozart as well as Stravinsky, so their counterparts in dance had to be equally at home with Petipa and Nijinska.

This, de Valois insisted, was true of the artists of the Diaghilev company, which she offered as a model to the English dance community. "Here," she wrote, "we have a repertory company running classical and modern ballet side by side—and what is more important—in many cases blended."[15]

At the heart of the article was a warning:

Dancers and dance students are now entering a new and important era—they are to be faced with the most serious task of all, that of establishing and safeguarding the methods of the true theorists on a solid foundation. Everyone knows what happens when an express train runs off the lines—the same disaster awaits an advancement in art that is not treated with intelligent care. The...theorists I have mentioned have countless imitators springing up on all sides, but they do not want imitators: they want disciples. One must see that the sincere work they have done towards the progress and expansion of ballet will not be swamped in time by enthusiastic but fundamentally inexperienced artists or [by] the criticisms of those who have no real understanding of their more advanced contemporaries.[16]

The implication was clear. As an experienced Diaghilev dancer, de Valois would be the intelligent caretaker of the "methods of the true theorists." She would build solidly on their foundations. The "future of ballet" in England might be glimpsed at her school and in the choreography that she now began to put before the public under the aegis of the repertory theater movement, which flourished in Britain in the 1920s.

This movement, explains Norman Marshall, a director and producer of the "other theater," was conceived as an alternative to the commercial productions that dominated the West End after the First World War. He traces the origins of the movement to the demise of the nineteenth-century actor-manager and the rise of a new breed of managers who demanded box office "hits" and "stars" capable of attracting a mass audience:

> Before 1914 the playgoer was served by managers running their own theatres according to their own taste and policy. Often the manager was also a distinguished actor, playing and producing in a theatre which he owned. During the war of 1914–18 theatres became just another asset on the list of properties held by business magnates, regarded as impersonally as the factories, the hotels, the chains of shops, the blocks of flats which also figured on the list. With the individual managers no longer in control, a frightful sameness descended upon the English theatre. The public was given what they wanted. At least, it seemed to be what they wanted, as theatres were packed, but they were given no chance of proving whether they wanted anything else.[17]

Like the Ballets Russes, which, as Lynn Garafola has shown, also had to adapt to a rapidly changing market in this period,[18] the repertory theater offered a combination of "classical" and "modern" plays. Works by Shakespeare, Marlowe, Ben Jonson, and Molière were juxtaposed with plays by Ibsen, Eugene O'Neill, Sean O'Casey, Jean Cocteau, and George Bernard Shaw—authors who were often regarded as controversial and as having little commercial appeal. Unlike Diaghilev, who managed to secure a place for the Ballets Russes in central London, the repertory theater developed in smaller venues away from the West End. The movement nurtured some of this century's finest actors, including John Gielgud, Laurence Olivier, Ralph Richardson, and Peggy Ashcroft, and it gave birth to what later became the National Theatre, an institution analogous to the Royal Ballet.

From the start de Valois saw her company as an integral part of the repertory theater movement. And from the first it was accepted as such by the theatrical community. In his history of the repertory theater movement Marshall devotes an entire chapter to the Sadler's Wells Ballet, placing it alongside the Old Vic, the Gate Theatre, and the Shakespeare Memorial Theatre at Stratford. He describes de Valois as one of the great creative minds of English theater, ranking her alongside George Bernard Shaw. It is worth quoting Marshall's assessment in full, for it indicates how her accomplishments were viewed by peers outside the dance world and to what extent her company was seen as a vital part of the renaissance of English theater:

> Creative genius in the theatre is rare. There is comparatively little scope for it. Actors and producers are not creators; they are interpreters of their

authors. During the period covered by this book the theatre discovered a number of intelligent, efficient authors, but since Shaw there has been none who could be described as a creative genius. One of the few figures which the theatre has produced during the period between the two wars to whom I would apply that description is Ninette de Valois. Choreography is a creative art, but I am not thinking of her as a choreographer when I describe Ninette de Valois as a creative genius, although creations such as *Job*, *The Rake's Progress* and *Checkmate* might with some justification be described as works of genius. It is of her work in creating a great English ballet company that I am thinking.[19]

Over the years de Valois worked in a number of theaters. But it was her collaboration with Terence Gray at the Festival Theatre in Cambridge, W. B. Yeats at the Abbey Theatre in Dublin, and Lilian Baylis at the Old Vic—that left a deep imprint on her choreography and her vision of English dance.

The Festival Theatre, where de Valois took her first job in the "other theater" in 1926, was one of the most exciting and visibly avant-garde institutions of the period. It was managed by Terence Gray, an Egyptologist turned theater man, who sank a fortune into the theater, which he opened in 1926 and managed until 1931. Gray also happened to be de Valois's cousin, but it was a shared sense of artistic purpose that brought them together. His vision of the theater was strongly influenced by Gordon Craig and Adolphe Appia, as well as by developments in continental drama. Gray built the Festival into one of the first modern alternatives to the proscenium stage in England. Norman Marshall, who worked with Gray, described it in his book about the repertory theater movement:

> At the Festival it was difficult to find any definite point at which the stage ended and the auditorium began. There was no proscenium. The width of the stage was the width of the auditorium itself. The broad forestage merging into a great fan-shaped flight of steps extending to the feet of the audience sitting in the front row abolished any boundary line between actor and audience.[20]

Marshall also suggests how the Festival stage opened up all sorts of new possibilities for the producer, actor, and director:

> Working at the Festival as a producer gave one an extraordinary sense of elbow room. The several levels provided by the stage, the forestage, and the steps gave opportunities for innumerable new combinations of movement and grouping impossible in an ordinary theatre where the actors would be masking one another. It was easy to get the actors on and off the stage without the elaborate and unnatural manoeuvres necessary on a picture-frame stage, as at the Festival in addition to the usual entrances there were two on the forestage, two more opening on to the steps from where in an ordinary theatre the stage boxes would be, and two more entrances down the gangways of the stalls on to the forestage steps. The upstage sec-

tion of the stage was constructed so as to roll forward giving access to the understage where a flight of steps provided yet further entrances, so that it was possible for an actor to walk straight up out of the back of the stage and instantly dominate the scene. An actor on the forestage or the steps was literally playing among the audience, for the auditorium itself was on the old Regency horseshoe plan, with curving balconies stretching on either side as far as the forestage itself.[21]

Gray was firmly opposed to conventional stage illusionism. He replaced realistic scenery and props with abstract constructions of various sizes that added not only to the visual interest of the stage but also to its space. Lighting was used to suggest changes of place and time. Like the stage, the lighting system was the most advanced at the time in England, allowing for numerous subtle changes in tone that could be coordinated with the movement of the actors and the scene changes.

Gray strongly believed that the traditional theater placed too much emphasis on the written text and not enough on the nonverbal aspects of a production. In his book *Dance-Drama: Experiments in the Art of the Theatre*, he railed with the zeal of a reformer against "the sovereignty of the spoken word." Once this had been "supreme in the theatre," he asserted, and "the solitary vehicle of drama"; now it was "but one of several factors, and must decrease in importance as the developing forces prove more efficient for the work."[22]

For Gray it was the expressive power of the stage itself that would destroy the "tyranny of words." He exulted in the revolution that had transformed scenic design:

> Artists of the theatre have so revolutionised and re-conceived stage machinery that by inspired construction of masses and by the skilled manipulation of the immensely powerful factor of coloured light, a medium of expression has been developed that is as potent, within its limitations, in the expression of dramatic realities and in the revelation of emotion as can ever be the words of a poet. Since science has delivered into the hands of the artist the immense possibilities of electricity as a medium of artistic expression a new view of the limitations of drama has become necessary. The result of this is that the words in which a play of the future shall be written shall have a less ubiquitous and exclusive part to play in the achievement of dramatic effect.[23]

Movement was an equally potent tool in the creation of dramatic effect, and it, too, encroached upon the "sovereignty of the spoken word," even "more threateningly," he felt, than lighting or scene design. For Gray, the plays of the future were plays in which "expressive" movement would assume an ever greater burden of the dramatic narrative.[24] In fact, Gray emphasized the importance of actor movement by calling his plays "dance dramas." He included several of these at the end of his book, including one, *The Scorpions of Ysit*, an "Egyptian fantasy dance" that de Valois later used as the basis of a ballet.[25] In his discussion of these dance-dramas, moreover, he devoted equal space to the written text, movement, and lighting effects. "Dancing," he explains,

> must be taken in its fullest meaning, must be understood to include all forms of studied movement, not the least of them studied immobility. It includes what is known as mime, it is mime rendered rhythmically, it is as verse to which mime is as prose, it is in fact every form of emotional expression by which the human-being can express himself, using his body as his medium.[26]

With fervor, he crusaded against traditional academic movement as this was exemplified in the *danse d'école*, finding pointework, especially, ludicrous and artificial. He greatly admired Fokine—the Fokine of *Petrouchka* and *Firebird*—whose theories on the nature of expressive dance movement were well known in the English theatrical community and who, like Gray himself, had been influenced by the Moscow Art Theater.[27] Gray was also deeply interested in the movement ideas linked to expressionist styles of acting on the continent, particularly in Central Europe.

It was to deal with "expressive actor movement" that Gray invited de Valois to join the staff as choreographer. Their collaboration began with the *Orestia*, the trilogy of Aeschylus plays that opened the theater in 1926. For this exciting production, de Valois "supplied a chorus made up of students" and "also arranged the choreography."[28] The music was by Donald Tovey and Gordon Jacob, the lighting by Harold Ridge, and the cast was headed by Maurice Evans, Miriam Lewis, and Hedley Briggs (who later danced for de Valois at the Old Vic and elsewhere).

Making good her assertion that the choreographer should be involved with all aspects of the production, de Valois worked closely with the noted classicist Robert C. Treveleyan, who had translated the plays. She studied the meter of classical poetry and integrated its rhythms into the movements of the actors. She also exploited the unusual configuration of the Festival Theatre stage and the fluid relationship it created between actors and audience: at one point, for instance, she had the Furies rush through the audience.

The choreography demonstrated her commitment to the new and "modern" movement vocabulary for which she had argued so eloquently in "The Future of the Ballet." Norman Marshall, who stage managed the production, recalled her work with admiration:

> Ninette de Valois' handling of the choruses was criticised because of the harshness and angularity of much of the movement. Certainly they had little in common with the soft flowing movements and gestures of the sentimentalized chorus to which the audiences were accustomed at that time. They had the beauty of strength and power, and although so uncompromisingly modernistic in manner they reproduced with perfect faithfulness the essential ritualistic quality of the Greek drama.[29]

At another point, Marshall linked her handling of the chorus with her later choreography for *Job*:

What Ninette de Valois achieved reduced one's memories of all other Greek choruses one had ever seen to a series of pretty posturings by comparison. It was not until five years later, when she created *Job*, that she again displayed the strength, the depth of feeling, the originality and dramatic force which characterised her handling of these choruses.[30]

The harsh, angular, and uncompromisingly modern movement that de Valois devised for the chorus reflected her interest in the gestural vocabulary of Central Europe. Gray's use of the phrase "expressive movement" reflected his attachment to a style that in England was often labeled "expressionism." The term was a translation of the French *expressionisme*, and after 1912, in Central Europe especially, it designated a broad range of artists associated with the avant-garde. Initially, the term was applied to the German antiacademic painters of Die Brücke (The Bridge) and Der Blau Reiter (The Blue Rider)—Ernst Kirchner, Emil Nolde, Wassily Kandinsky, Oskar Kokoschka—themselves strongly influenced by the French fauves.[31] Within the dance world, expressionism as a term was most often used to describe what became known in England in the second half of the 1920s as "Central European dance." Embracing the eurhythmic techniques of Dalcroze and the movement choirs of Laban (as well as a number of other influences), Central European dance was viewed as an alternative to the *danse d'école*. Typically performed in bare feet or soft shoes, it was characterized by a freer use of the arms than in the classical school, a flexible, articulate torso, an often highly emphatic gestural vocabulary, and a tendency toward angularity.

How did this influence seep into de Valois's work? There wasn't all that much Central European dance to see in England. P.J.S. Richardson, who, as editor and chief critic of *The Dancing Times*, made it his business to see everything, later dated "the commencement of interest in Central European movement" from 1928, when Mary Wigman made her first appearance in London on a Sunshine Matinee program shared with Ashton, de Valois, and others.[32] But this was two years after the *Orestia* and one year after de Valois choreographed her strongly expressionistic ballet *Rout*. In England, at least, she had preceded Wigman.

As a member of the Ballets Russes, de Valois had visited Switzerland, Holland, and Germany, countries where she could have observed examples of the new choreography. However, the breathless pace of Diaghilev's tours would have precluded an extended acquaintance with its forms.

Some Central European ideas had been with de Valois since her days at Mrs. Wordsworth's school, where eurhythmics had been part of the curriculum. In coordinating the movement of the actors in the *Orestia* with the rhythmic structure of Treveleyan's text, she may well have used certain eurhythmic techniques. Then, too, Nijinska's work at this time—and that of other Diaghilev choreographers, especially Massine—revealed the "harshness," angularity, and use of masses associated with trends emanating from Central Europe.

Whenever, and wherever she saw it, Central European dance had a powerful impact on de Valois's style. She viewed its "revolutionary tendencies," however, not as an alternative to classicism, but as an enrichment of it, discoveries to be absorbed into ballet's living, renewable tradition. In her 1937 book *Invitation to the Ballet*, written after the impact of Wigman had been strikingly felt in England, de Valois expressed her esteem for Wigman, calling her an "artist and mind of importance." However, she went on to argue that Wigman's "creation," like Martha Graham's, was "based on a destruction *of* rather than an evolution *from* what has gone before."[33] These expressionist influences, in combination with ideas absorbed from Diaghilev's choreographers, gave a strikingly modern look to de Valois's movement vocabulary. Indeed, in England of the 1920s she was among the first—if not *the* first—to exploit the expressionist vein of modern dance.

This "ultra modern" style (as Richardson called it) was vividly displayed in the ballet *Rout*, first performed at the Festival Theatre on 31 January 1927. Before this, de Valois's "new" choreography had mainly appeared in the context of plays. Now, with students from her Academy of Choregraphic Art, she created a full-fledged dance work combining movement, music, and the spoken word. The opening section was performed in soft shoes (later in bare feet) to a poem by Ernst Toller. In the following section, to music by Arthur Bliss arranged for two pianos, the vocal accompaniment—composed for Grace Lovat Fraser—consisted, as Fraser wrote, of "only meaningless syllables chosen for their colour values and percussive or soft impact."[34]

The choice of Toller and Bliss acknowledged the two major influences on de Valois at this time—Central European expressionism and Ballets Russes modernism. Toller, a German poet, dramatist, and pacifist, stood at the forefront of the expressionist movement in German theater. (He would later write the scenario for Kurt Jooss's prize-winning ballet, *The Green Table*.) Toller was introduced to London audiences in 1923 by Ashley Dukes, who had translated his play *The Machine Wreckers*. Dukes, who was the husband of Marie Rambert and thus an acquaintance of de Valois, had also translated the Toller poem she used in *Rout*; indeed, he may well have suggested it to her. Bliss's music had been performed as a musical interlude on a Ballets Russes program in London, and Kathrine Sorley Walker suggests that it was in this context that de Valois probably first heard it.[35]

As Richardson later described it, *Rout* was a ballet about "the revolt of modern youth against the conventions of the older generation…built up of decorative groupings and 'futuristic' movement, frequently of a contrapuntal nature."[36] According to *The Times*, the movements were "based on those of fly-wheels and piston-rods, synchronised with the music, the rhythm being emphasized by the beating of the dancers' feet."[37] Ashton, who danced in the 1931 production given by the Camargo Society, recalled the counts as being complex and difficult to remember.[38] The

A scene from Rout. The Dancing Times, *January 1933, p. 437.*

combination of mass groupings, contrapuntal movement, and intricate rhythms stressed by footwork suggests that, even more than Central European trends, it is Nijinska's influence that pervades the ballet, especially her choreography for *Les Noces*.

Rout was an important ballet for de Valois, so much so that she arranged a London performance of the work a year after its Festival premiere. This special performance took place at the Academy of Choreographic Art before an invited public that included some of de Valois's strongest supporters: Lydia Lopokova, Richardson, and the music critic Edwin Evans. Adding to the atmosphere was the presence of the composer and Malcolm Sargeant at the pianos.

Movement, which de Valois choreographed for Anton Dolin and Phyllis Bedells around the time of *Rout*, was another ballet in her new style, although this time pointework was used. Reviewing the work, Richardson noted its "cleavage from the old methods" and the influence of Nijinska's *Les Biches* on some of the movements of the choreography.[39]

Richardson featured the two ballets prominently in his February 1928 editorial column, which he used to usher in the new year in dance and reflect on the old. He characterized 1927 as a turning point for British ballet. "This past year seems to have been spent in endeavouring to find some form of movement which does express the spirit of the present age, and generally this has been done by substituting straight lines and angles for the curves of the classic period."[40] He went on to write respectfully about the London performance of *Rout*, describing the ballet as a "notable" experiment that showed de Valois to be "a real, honest enquirer into the possibilities of the dance as a mode of interpreting modern thought." He expressed the hope that *Rout* would be repeated on a "proper" stage, so the "pattern" of the dance could be seen to better effect. And, cannily, he let his readers know that the ballet—and, by extension, its choreographer—had received the support of one of London's most popular Ballets Russes stars. "Madame Lopokova was an interested spectator," he observed, "and I noticed she was one of the most enthusiastic applauders."[41]

Richardson's public endorsement of *Rout* and de Valois's wish to present it to important critics and friends in the ballet world reveals a major difference in the development of modern forms of dance in England and the United States. In subject and style, *Rout* (or *Rituelle de Feu*, choreographed in 1928) would not have been out of place among the group works created in the 1930s by American modern dancers, especially works (such as Graham's *Panorama*) that were indebted to expressionism. What differed was the artistic context that gave these works cultural meaning. For Graham and most of her colleagues, modern dance was inherently revolutionary not only because of its movement idiom but also because of its ideological stance, which was often explicitly leftist. Hence, their scorn for ballet, which they viewed as detrimental to the development of modern dance, and a potential source, even, of its artistic and ideological contamination. The new art demanded a new school. For de Valois, on the other hand, the techniques and themes of the new dance could easily be absorbed into the ballet repertory, where a variety of styles and idioms could—and should—coexist, as they did in the concert hall and repertory theater.[42]

De Valois continued her choreographic experiments at the Festival Theatre in both plays and short dance pieces. The cycle of Greek plays continued with productions of Sophocles's *Oedipus the King* and *Antigone*, Aeschylus's *Prometheus*, and Aristophanes's comedy *The Birds*, which was presented as a modern musical comedy. She also choreographed the movement and dances for a number of Shakespeare plays, including *As You Like It*, *Henry VIII*, and *Richard III*. In the dream scene on Bosworth's Field, where Richard sees the ghosts of his victims, she made effective use of the Festival's sophisticated lighting system, so that, in the words of one critic, the "seemingly endless procession of...gyrating figures, their gaunt arms outstretched in an appeal for vengeance, set monstrous purple shadows looming over the cyclorama."[43] She also staged the Dance of the Seven Veils for a private performance of Oscar Wilde's *Salomé*, which was then banned in England.

The dance programs that de Valois choreographed for the Festival Theatre were performed by her students from the Academy of Choregraphic Art. In these short pieces she experimented extensively with floorwork and also with eurhythmic techniques. In *Rhythm*, the dancers never rose from the floor, while the movements of their arms, heads, and torsos reflected the musical rhythm and structure. The floorwork in *Pois-*

A scene from Rituelle de Feu. *Photo by Independent Newspapers, Ltd.* The Dancing Times,
March 1933, p. 668.

sons d'Or, to Debussy, was also inventive: at one point she had the
dancers wriggle along the floor like fish. And she used modern music,
choosing pieces by Ravel, Poulenc, and Debussy that revealed Diaghilev's
continued sway over her imagination. His influence was reinforced by the
advice of the music critic Edwin Evans, a friend and passionate advocate
of twentieth-century music.

At the Festival Theatre, *Rout* had received its premiere on a program
that included *On Baile's Strand* by William Butler Yeats. De Valois created the movement for the play and also worked closely with the director,
Norman Marshall, on the lighting, a subtle, ever-changing combination of
blues and greens evoking mist and sea. As in other Festival productions,
steps and platforms were used to create various stage levels, while huge
pillars suggested the great hall at Dundealgan, where Yeats had set his tale
of the legendary Irish hero Cuchulain. The ritual movement, partly
inspired by the masks designed by Hedley Briggs for the Blind Man and
the Fool, testified yet again to her interest in forceful, stylized, and angular gesture.

The poet Gordon Bottomley, who was in the audience on opening
night, spoke highly of her work to Yeats, and when the poet came to
Cambridge in May 1927 to see a performance of his play *The Player
Queen*, he made a point of attending a matinee program that included
Rhythm, Poissons d'Or, and other works in the style of her "new choreography." Yeats was so impressed that he invited de Valois to work with
him at the Abbey Theatre in Dublin. He wanted her to stage his Plays for
Dancers, an enterprise that he had abandoned more than a decade before,
when Michio Ito, the Japanese dancer with whom he was then collaborat-

ing, left for America; he also wanted her to create a school at the Abbey to train dancers. With her help, Yeats said, "the poetic drama of Ireland would live again and take its rightful place in the nation's own theatre."[44] De Valois was intrigued. She loved poetry and also wrote it, and she was still deeply attached to her native land. So, she added the Abbey to an already full list of responsibilities. Another important phase of her career had opened.

"A Strange, Noble, Unforgettable Figure": De Valois, Yeats, Baylis, and Rambert

These are Yeats's words, and they describe de Valois as she appeared in 1929 in *Fighting the Waves*, the first ballet play they did together at Dublin's Abbey Theatre.[1]

Yeats had been "very moved" by his first glimpse of her work at the Festival Theatre, and it awakened in him a resolve to revive his Plays for Dancers with de Valois as their choreographer and featured dancer. He insisted on meeting de Valois the morning after the Festival performance. De Valois was deeply touched by this encounter with the poet, which she vividly described fifty years later in *Step by Step*:

> We met the next morning in the dim foyer of the theatre. Always I can recall the great dark figure sitting in profile. Yeats had a curious habit of not looking at his companion during a conversation. He would look down or up or remain, as in this case, in profile. The voice was warm, rich with a mighty resonance of its own. He always conversed with conviction and inspiration, and you remained unperturbed that you were not included in his line of vision.

"A Strange, Noble, Unforgettable Figure": de Valois (second from left) as Fand in Fighting the Waves, *Abbey Theatre, 1929. To her left: Hedley Briggs as the Ghost of Cuchulain, Michael Dolan as Cuchulain, and Merial Moore (with dagger) as Emer. Photo by Graphic Studios, Dublin. The Dancing Times, September 1929, p. 542.*

> I could see before the conversation had started that he had come to a decision and that it was for me to listen and accept, and then to be led. The opening was both simple and direct: "I want you to come to Dublin to help me revive my Plays for Dancers which now must be restaged and put back into the Dublin scene"....
>
> The idea filled me with both joy and excitement, for I had a veneration for Ireland's National Theatre. He went on to tell me that he thought that...the Abbey was in a groove, he wanted to see poetic drama encouraged, to establish something that was far removed from the conventional plays that they were endlessly performing.[2]

At the Abbey, de Valois continued her exploration of the relationship between words and movement begun with the *Oresteia* and *Rout*, but with a new emphasis. In contrast to Terence Gray, who took a genuine interest in all the arts, Yeats, she recalled,

> had always felt the call of movement in relation to his writings, and he felt the same draw towards music. But he did not show any active interest in music and dance as arts in their own right. For him it was the call of the rhythm of the body, and the musicality of words, the search for a fusion in a unified expression of his dance dramas, symbolic in the oneness of the mystery that surrounded his great vision.[3]

Tragically, there is no detailed record of how de Valois explored the relationship between the "rhythm of the body" and "the musicality of words" in her work with Yeats. (Kathrine Sorley Walker has collected what little descriptive material exists from contemporary reviews.)[4] But Yeats was clearly happy with the collaboration: not only did he revive the Plays for Dancers for her, he also wrote a prose version of *The Only Jealousy of Emer* for her (this was *Fighting the Waves*) and a new work, *The King of the Great Clock Tower* (1934), which he dedicated to her, "asking pardon for covering her expressive face with a mask."[5] And he was deeply disappointed when, because of other commitments, she had to leave the Abbey.

The affinity between the Irish poet and choreographer stemmed not only from their shared nationality but also from their common love of poetry. De Valois loved poetry and had written it since she was a child first exploring her grandmother's great library. Although never anything but an avocation, it remained a serious and significant part of her life. Indeed, writing poetry was her habitual response to particularly moving situations. "Dancers in Action," a poem recording her deep and stirring response to Kenneth MacMillan's *Song of the Earth*, concludes her book of essays *Step by Step*, and a collection of her poems, *The Cycle*, covering a wide range of topics—London urban life, nature, pubs, age—was published in 1985 in aid of Sadler's Wells.[6] Written in a variety of forms, including free verse, de Valois's poems are amateur in the truest sense of the word: she is a real lover of the art. Influenced by modernism but infused with a romantic sensibility, they suggest more than describe, evoke rather than recreate, and depend in large part on the musicality of the words and the rhythms of the phrases for their power.

De Valois's approach to Yeats was intuitive rather than intellectual. As she describes it, her task in creating movement for the enigmatic universe of his plays was not so much to understand his words as to "feel" their meaning. For someone with such a powerful intellect and a "thinky," analytical approach to things—this, after all, was the same woman who had written down all her lessons with Espinosa, organized, and analyzed them—it must have been a daunting task to work with Yeats. As abundantly demonstrated in her writings, explanation and analysis come naturally to de Valois. Indeed, they are two of her greatest talents and the key to her genius as an organizer. In her discussion of Yeats's plays, by contrast, we encounter the poetic and intuitive side of her personality that has usually been overlooked. As she wrote in *Step by Step*:

> Time and time again I have been asked to analyse and give a picture of what these productions were like. It is almost an impossible task. I can state, though, that you had to feel more than understand; you had to allow yourself to be absorbed into the whole, never to exist as an isolated part, only as a part of the whole. It became more and more a question of feeling the play rather than intellectually trying to understand every line. In the end there was a fusion; you felt your body and your emotions take part in the spirit of the general production. There was its intense simplicity, its purity, the direct appeal to feeling and its poetry. I gave up trying to understand many moments, instead I accepted and became absorbed. In certain passages I was reminded of the poet's own words:
>
> > I have bid you turn
> > From the cavern of the mind[7]

"Much...discussion," she says at another point, "has been devoted to [Yeats's] 'symbolism' and 'mysticism'":

> Dare I say perhaps, interesting and significant as this aspect of the poet is known to be, the whole matter is being somewhat overplayed? We are in danger, I feel, of not being able to see the wood for the trees. A great poet sings to us from his heart, and how this heart arrives at all the wonderment that it finds is a matter of vision; it has more strength left alone, left wrapped in its own mystery, and he would mean us to absorb the ultimate with the accent on a sublime and contented acceptance of any one of his sequence of words. That he wrote of his experience did not mean the necessity of a prolonged and painful analysis of how he may or may not have applied them to his poetry.[8]

For the Abbey plays and for the other works she did there, de Valois again drew on the vocabulary of Central European dance and the modernist legacy of the Ballets Russes. In *The Faun* (1928), a ballet to tradi-

A scene from The Faun. *Photo by McNally, Dublin.* The Dancing Times, *February 1930, p. 565.*

tional Irish music arranged by Harold R. White, the use of bare feet, parallel stance, dense masses, and frieze-style lines recalled ballets by Nijinsky and Nijinska as well as Central European choral movement. Now, however, a new influence appeared in her work, that of Japanese Noh drama, in which Yeats had long been interested. Noting the "extreme simplicity" of productions at the Abbey, she wrote that

> [a]t certain moments the scene would become completely static. I had already noted the wonderful coordination between the players in the theatre's straight plays. In these Plays for Dancers the production merely highlighted this strange sense of interplay, and this is also evident in the Noh plays of Japan, although their technical approach with its ageless tradition is more involved. This gift of Celtic understatement proved to be masterly when a work included music, words, song and dance.[9]

As Valois suggests, the emphasis on extreme simplicity, stillness, and close interplay among the performers in the Abbey plays was also characteristic of Noh drama. Another link between the two was the enigmatic nature of the plot. As William P. Malm explains in his study of Japanese music:

[I]f one compares [Noh] with Western drama, it often seems to be lacking any real plot line. Nothing seems to have happened by the end of the play, and the two acts frequently have little connection. This could be explained by comparing the plays with the tea ceremony, which developed concurrently with noh. The purpose of both the play and the ceremony lies not in the form but in the objects presented and the atmosphere created. In either case, one should not seek only an intellectual understanding but rather savor the highly specialized aesthetic experience. It must be remembered that the influence of Zen Buddhism, with its love of allusions and emphasis of non-logical procedures, was strong when noh was developed.

In noh everything is restrained in an attempt to produce as pure an aesthetic atmosphere as possible. If one approaches a noh play looking for the Western concepts of extensive plot development or strong character delineations and interrelations, many plays will seem very poor indeed.[10]

Japanese Noh and Central European expressionist influence also stand behind de Valois's use of masks, another prominent stylizing feature of her work at the Abbey Theatre. Although one critic described the masks in *Fighting the Waves* as making the performers look like a "collection of battered nursery dolls,"[11] de Valois was fascinated and challenged by them, and her use of masks in several productions belies yet again the myth of her conservative, unadventurous nature as an artist. "In these plays," she wrote,

Hedley Briggs as the Ghost of Cuchulain with students from the Abbey school in Fighting the Waves, *Abbey Theatre, 1929. Photo by Graphic Studios, Dublin.* The Dancing Times, *September 1929, p. 542.*

one developed a very strange and moving reaction to the poet, the strength of the stilled mind, devoid of anything but the purity of deep inner meaning that was not capable of expression in the concrete terms of everyday speech. It was not the theatre that I knew, there was none of the theatrical effects, theatrical approaches that I was used to.... There was no tortuous breakdown ordering you to return to the cavern of the mind and turn it into a research laboratory. Again to find a parallel we recall the Noh players.

We played in masks, both actors and dancers. Here was a nobility of form that added to the remote objective feeling of the whole venture, for the mask was the outward and important symbol of this inner force that was at work. My mask never worried me, for its presence became all-important. They were beautiful masks and caught the spirit of the poet's dream world. I always studied my masks very carefully and then I knew what I had to express with my movements so as to illustrate both action and meaning. In the end I just felt that my face was a part of the mask's own projection.[12]

As much as de Valois liked and learned working at the Abbey, her days there were numbered. Her hopes for the future lay in England and in her growing success at Sadler's Wells Theatre. In 1934, to Yeats's great disappointment, she left the Abbey to devote herself entirely to building a company at Sadler's Wells. Here, in collaboration with Lilian Baylis, the second remarkable woman who would serve as a powerful role model for de Valois, she created the repertory dance company that would be the true cradle of modern British ballet.

When de Valois first met her, Baylis was fifty-two and entering the last decade of her life.[13] Born in London in 1874 to musician parents, she was a child prodigy, making her debut as a violinist at the age of nine. In 1891, the family moved to South Africa, where she became one of the first teachers of European music in Johannesburg. Six years later, she returned to London to assist her aunt, Emma Cons, a social reformer, who ran the Royal Victoria Hall and Coffee Tavern to provide affordable entertainment in an alcohol-free environment for the working-class people who lived in the neighborhood. This later became the Old Vic. Baylis, following in her aunt's footsteps, combined a fervent religious faith and a social worker's commitment to the betterment of the working classes with a love of drama and music. She would devote the rest of her life to developing people's theaters at the Old Vic and Sadler's Wells that would make serious repertory theater (especially Shakespeare), "grand" opera, and ballet available to working-class communities at popular prices.[14] She was "possessed," wrote de Valois,

with the fervour of a Salvation Lass of her period. Her banner took the form of the famous green leaflets that we were asked to "mislay" in buses and tubes. At one time she marched through the streets of Lambeth and Islington distributing the leaflets at various houses. She would tell the occupants that she had something both beautiful and respectable to give to the general public, and that she had the support and approval of the Lord.[15]

Baylis put her faith in de Valois's vision of a repertory dance company and ability to develop one at a time when such a thing was unheard of. How important this acceptance and approval were to de Valois can be gauged by the number of times she recounted their first meeting. Like her first hearing of Nijinska's *Les Noces*, the moment is emblazoned on her memory as a decisive turning point in her life. The encounter took place in 1926, shortly after de Valois had opened her Academy of Choregraphic Art. She was in search of a stage, a home for her dancers within the repertory theater movement. In *Step by Step* she offered one of her most vivid recollections of the event:

> My first interview with her was in the summer of 1926. That year I wrote two special letters. They contained the outline of a possible scheme for starting an English Ballet in a repertory theatre. I forwarded one to the Old Vic and the other to the Birmingham Repertory Theatre. The Birmingham Theatre turned the project down—but the management of the Old Vic sent for me.
>
> By a curious coincidence Miss Baylis was looking for someone to take charge of her dramatic students' weekly dancing class, and to be responsible for the arrangement of any short dances in the plays. The interview was characteristic. She had my letter in her hand—and said that she thought it showed enthusiasm coupled with a practical mind. She thought I had enough experience to know my job, and that she liked my face—but had never heard of me professionally. She added that she had been told I was a good dancer—but did not consider that she held any proof, as yet, of my teaching ability, in fact I might be quite hopeless with her drama students. She suggested coming with her producer...to my private studio to see me give my students a lesson. She came—approved and engaged me to do the only work there was to be done at the time. She promised me, that as time went on and things got better, my more ambitious plans would receive her full consideration, and the eventual building of Sadler's Wells would mean the opening of a school in that building, and the nucleus of a ballet installed within its walls.[16]

De Valois goes on to say that "from here on I have memories of her continual uphill struggle and a recollection of being dragged along a path that seemed full of insurmountable difficulties." Nonetheless, the two women succeeded, and though at first Baylis could only give de Valois work coaching actors in movement and choreographing dances in plays and operas at the Old Vic, when Sadler's Wells finally opened, the beginnings of a ballet company was indeed "installed within its walls."

Baylis's conception of theater as a means of uplifting and enriching the lives of the working people who lived in the neighborhood surrounding

Sadler's Wells would have a powerful impact on de Valois's conception of her company, its role in the lives of its audience, and the position of its dancers. De Valois may have first learned about state-supported ballet from her colleagues in the Diaghilev company, but it was from Baylis that she absorbed the nineteenth-century philanthropic idea that the arts could and should enrich the lives of people of all classes, not just a privileged elite. Islington, where Sadler's Wells Theatre was located, was a predominantly working-class neighborhood. Rows of early Victorian working-class dwellings lined the streets adjoining the theater. Although parts of the area have become gentrified, it remains, even today, a mixed neighborhood.

In her 1937 book *Invitation to the Ballet*, a brilliant assessment of ballet's past and a forecast of its future, de Valois insisted that the repertory theater movement (of which she saw her company as part) was "as vital to the welfare of the community as the hospital."[17] Even more tellingly, she goes on to characterize "those…assisting in the important Repertory Movement in the English theatre" as "upholding one of the orthodox necessities of life":

> For the highest forms of the theatre are a part of life's necessities and should be accepted as a part of the order of things that constitute the world one lives in. [This] is not an imaginative idealism; on the contrary, it conjures up a practical issue of an ideal based on reason. A universal Utopia may never exist, but always has it been present in isolated makings and endeavours. Thus it is something to be concerned with isolated standards worthy of recognition, and to endeavour to consolidate their positions.[18]

These "isolated" bits of utopia, she argued, should be made available at affordable prices to members of *all* classes, just as those who worked in the theater should be paid a living wage. "It is essential," she wrote, "for the Repertory Theatre movement in England to stabilise itself as the State theatre. It should be run as a well-controlled business of an important social order, carefully stocked with self-respecting wage-earners."[19] Patrons of the "Wells" could see these "self-respecting wage-earners" performing Shakespeare, Ashton, and Verdi for as little as sixpence, the price of a seat in the gallery. This was Baylis's vision, and de Valois made it her own. In fact, de Valois sometimes used the term "repertory" and "people's" theater interchangeably, nowhere more tellingly than in her assertion that "the gallery, the pit, and the amphitheatre"—that is, the cheapest parts of the house—"are the backbone of the repertory or people's theatre."[20] Another statement in *Invitation to the Ballet* sums up this democratic vision: "the theatre proper, like the principles of Christianity, is a necessary part of the world's general sanity. It may well be honoured and supported by the rich, understood and lived on by the people, and that true bourgeoisie which make up the greater part of any country's population."[21]

The birth and growth of de Valois's company within the context of Baylis's theater and opera companies, and the repertory theater movement as a whole, left an indelible mark on the nature and character of British ballet and shaped the attitude of its teachers, choreographers, dancers, critics, and audiences for decades to come. With dance evenings alternating with performances of plays and operas of every variety, the ballet company and its director (herself an employee of the Baylis organization) saw themselves very much as part of a larger whole and very much a part of the world of the theater. No matter what the period, ballets were conceived as dance dramas. This was true not only of "story" ballets with carefully plotted narratives, but also of works that were more abstract and poetic in nature, conveying a general mood or atmosphere. Dancers were actors, and acting was seen as an integral part of their training: indeed, at Sadler's Wells, the dancers worked alongside a brilliant constellation of players including Laurence Olivier, John Gielgud, and Ralph Richardson. Some productions even shared personnel, as when Elsa Lanchester performed the Arabian dance in the first Vic-Wells production of *The Nutcracker*,[22] or, later, when Robert Helpmann moved from dance to drama. Mime, too, was considered an essential part of the dancer's training, and to teach the repertory of traditional Italian gestures de Valois hired Francesca Zanfretta, a former "première mime" at the Empire Theatre who had studied in Milan in the 1870s. With her usual thoroughness, de Valois wrote these gestures down and incorporated them into the curriculum of her school.

Thus, a dancer's ability to act as well as to move became a hallmark of British training, and audiences and critics regarded the two skills as inseparable. A dancer, no matter how technically proficient, was only considered to be truly accomplished if he or she could develop subtle and detailed characterizations blending movement and expression. This skill became a hallmark of the British dancer. So, too, did the close interplay that transformed the individuals onstage into a unified ensemble of dancer-actors. Finally, as in a repertory theater company, where actors might play Shakespeare one night and Shaw or Yeats the next, the dancers of de Valois's company had to move with ease from narrative to more abstract forms and to adapt to a range of period styles.

These same abilities were being asked of another group of dancers who also shared a venue with a London theater company, albeit one far from the working-class "suburb" of Islington where Sadler's Wells was located. This was the Ballet Club, founded by Marie Rambert and operated in tandem with her husband Ashley Dukes, the director of the Mercury Theatre. Located in Notting Hill Gate, the Mercury was close to the tree-lined streets and stately homes of Holland Park and Kensington.

In her autobiography *Quicksilver*, Rambert says that she and de Valois were often mistaken for another, although de Valois "was much younger and had much better features. She told me she was often addressed as Madame Rambert, and many times people addressed me by her name."[23]

Marie Rambert and Ashley Dukes at the entrance to the Mercury Theatre auditorium. Photo by Tom L. Blau. Rambert Dance Company Archives.

De Valois confirms that this was indeed the case. "It happened," she once told me bemusedly, "all the time."[24]

Perhaps, with hindsight, this confusion can be explained. Although they came from entirely different worlds, spoke with different accents, and differed in age, taste, temperament, and talent, de Valois and Rambert shared a single passionate aim to which they devoted themselves with all the force of their formidable personalities. This aim was the development and establishment of a British dance organization consisting of native choreographers and dancers, an organization of international standing viewed in the eyes of the world as the equal of any major ballet company. As leaders of the dominant dance organizations in England, both were seen as the "mothers" of British ballet.

Of course, de Valois and Rambert shared another trait in common, and this may be the fundamental reason for the confusion. They were both women in visible positions of authority in a society in which most institutions were run by men. Both had powerful and, at times, ferocious personalities. Given the enormity of the problems they faced, they certainly needed them. In addition to the obstacles placed in their way by a society largely indifferent to dance as an art form, both had to deal with societal expectations of women's roles. De Valois tells a story about registering, as all British subjects were required to do, for war work during the Second World War:

> In my forty-fourth year my age-group was called up. I was in the North with the Ballet and went to register there. A woman, wearing the expression of someone bidden to sit on one ice-block, and lean back against another, rapped out her questions. In one minute she had discovered many things: that I was married; that my husband was a busy doctor; that the surgery was a part of our private house; that the Ministry of Labour allowed us one maid; that I was employed by the Governors of Sadler's Wells as director of the Ballet; that I had to go home every week-end to attend to the duties of a doctor's house and let my maid have the Sunday off. She then asked if I had any children, and as the answer was in the negative, announced, with enormous finality, that I came under the category of no responsibilities. The tip of her long, masterful pencil pointed to the printed question "Have you any responsibilities?" With arctic politeness she instructed me to write "None". I did so.[25]

Rambert must have encountered similar situations. Yet in the face of all this, the two succeeded; in de Valois's case, even beyond her wildest expectations. They were the first women in twentieth-century Britain to have a critical, indeed revolutionary impact on the country's arts organizations. Not only did they change the face of British dance, they also made a place—a central place—for dance in the British arts panorama. Through the dancers and the choreographers they formed and the works they brought to fruition, they influenced the development of ballet internationally. And if one adds to this the national organizations founded by former de Valois dancers in Canada (Celia Franca), Australia (Peggy van Praagh and Robert Helpmann), Germany (John Cranko), and Turkey (Beatrice Appleyard), the legacy is in fact astounding.

In most ways, however, the two women were dissimilar. For one thing, they came from different worlds. Rambert, although married to an Englishman and thus a naturalized British subject, was a foreigner, and this status and her foreign accent must have worked both for and against her. Born Cyvia Rambam in Warsaw in 1888, she was ten years older than de Valois. Inspired as a teenager by Isadora Duncan (after a performance in Warsaw she invaded the dancer's dressing room, vowing allegiance and kissing her feet!), Rambert began her career as an interpretative or "art" dancer. In 1905, at her family's behest, she went to Paris to study medicine, but instead immersed herself in dance, becoming part of Raymond Duncan's circle and dancing à la Isadora at society parties. In 1909[26] she attended a summer holiday course on eurhythmics at Emile Jaques-Dalcroze's institute in Geneva: intending to stay for ten days, she remained with the school for three years, moving with it to Hellerau, teaching, and appearing with Dalcroze's hand-picked group of demonstration dancers.

When Diaghilev consulted Dalcroze with the intention of hiring someone to help Nijinsky cope with the music for *The Rite of Spring*, Dalcroze recommended Rambert. Joining the Ballets Russes in December 1912, Rambert spent the next year working closely with Nijinsky and dancing in the corps de ballet, appearing not only in *Rite* but also in various Fokine works and even in *Swan Lake* and *Giselle*, although not in roles that demanded classical technique. In the Diaghilev company, she began working on a daily basis with Cecchetti, and gradually her prejudice against ballet was replaced by love. But she continued to admire modern styles of dance, and the new paths in ballet opened by Nijinsky and Fokine.

When Diaghilev and Nijinsky parted ways in 1913, Rambert's services were no longer needed. She returned to Paris to study and perform. In 1914 she went to London and took classes with Serafima Astafieva, whom she knew from the Diaghilev company. In 1917 she met the English playwright and drama critic Ashley Dukes, and after a brief courtship they were married in 1918. Later that year she resumed classes with Cecchetti, who had temporarily settled in London: it may have been at his studio that she first got to know de Valois. In 1920, the year she received her

Cecchetti teaching certificate, she opened a small school, and in 1926, with her pupils, presented *A Tragedy of Fashion*, the first ballet by her student Frederick Ashton and her friend, the designer Sophie Fedorovitch. Four years later, she founded the Ballet Club, which, beginning in 1931, shared the premises of the newly opened Mercury Theatre with her husband's theater company. By this time, she and Dukes had settled near the theater in Holland Park.

However different in background and training from de Valois, Rambert, too, was powerfully influenced by Diaghilev and his conception of ballet. That de Valois joined the Ballets Russes at all may have had something to do with Rambert. At the memorial service for Rambert, de Valois told the story of how during one of Cecchetti's classes, it was announced that she had been invited to join the Diaghilev company. She must have looked hesitant about the offer, because when class was over Rambert dashed breathlessly down the corridor after her, exclaiming with all the force of her voluble personality: "You must go! It will change your life!"[27]

Whether because of this incident or for other reasons, de Valois felt genuinely grateful to Rambert. She publicly acknowledged her gratitude in 1937 when she dedicated *Invitation to the Ballet* jointly to Rambert and Lilian Baylis—the most important women in her life at that time. A letter written shortly before the publication of the book reveals de Valois's deep affection and respect for "Mim" (as Rambert was known familiarly to friends):

> My dear Mim,
>
> Have I your permission to dedicate my book jointly to you and Miss Baylis? I fully realise it is a difficult thing to say no—and that you may live to wish you had not said yes. But I don't see how I can help you, any more than I am going to be able to help a number of people thinking that the book should never have been written at all—at the moment my own reaction! But all these reasonings will not stop me asking you to accept—if you feel under any circumstances that you can survive the possible risk.
>
> Yours affectionately,
> Ninette[28]

Although dedicated to Rambert, *Invitation to the Ballet* suggests perhaps the biggest difference between the two women: the ability to conceptualize, articulate, and implement both long and short-term goals. As her book makes amply clear, this was de Valois's greatest strength. She could plan ahead—not only from season to season, but even more remarkably for events that lay five and ten years in the future—and she could persuade—not just with charm, like Rambert, who could be extremely charming—but with the force and logic of an articulate writer. Rambert, as she herself acknowledged, was just the opposite. Looking back over her career in 1974, she told John Gruen: "If there is one person who has no foresight, it's me. ... Everything for me happens at the moment."[29]

> I didn't form a company with any idea of forming [it]. All my life, whatever I did, was purely instinctive.... That's why I made so many messes. So often I messed things up because,... no sooner did an idea come to me than I acted upon it without any judgment whatsoever.... And thank God, somehow it seems to have turned out not so badly. But actually I had no idea of forming a company.[30]

And elsewhere:

> It's extraordinary, when I look back on all my life, how unplanned it was. I was incapable of making any plan whatsoever. My husband [took care of] all my practical life. He arranged [it].... I could teach, but I couldn't prepare a lesson. I could correct a ballet, but I had to see it.... It seems to me quite extraordinary that I cannot plan. [P]robably, I would have done great things if I could plan.[31]

As the *Bar aux Folies-Bergère* notebook reveals, de Valois thought everything out beforehand. Like the letter she fired off to Lilian Baylis and the Birmingham Repertory Theatre in 1926 and the article she wrote for *The Dancing Times* in the same year, *Invitation to the Ballet* outlines a strategy for the future of ballet in England. Arnold Haskell recalls talking one day to "Madam" (as company members frequently called her), and noticing that she seemed preoccupied, asked what was on her mind. To his amazement, she answered that she was thinking about the kind of bedding for the boys at the company school five years from then![32]

This aspect of de Valois's personality, along with her self-assured manner could be intimidating. (Actually, de Valois was less self-assured than she appeared. She once told me that she still felt like an impostor and was waiting for everyone to "find me out.")[33] Among those intimidated was Rambert. She attended the opening of the Academy of Choregraphic Art in 1926, and was photographed along with de Valois and other honored guests, including Lydia Lopokova, Edwin Evans, and Anton Dolin. The event left her profoundly depressed. As she recalled in *Quicksilver*:

> In 1926 Ninette de Valois opened her Academy of Choregraphic [sic] Art in London. I thought the name of the school too grandiloquent, but the prospectus impressed me very much. It showed great intelligence, immense knowledge of ballet and the theatre, as well as practical sense, and seemed to carry in it a promise of future great developments. It made me feel very small and ignorant and useless. I seriously thought that I should send all my pupils to Ninette and close my school. My depression grew every day until Ashley became quite impatient with my moaning and threatened to go to America for six months.[34]

De Valois was also a choreographer who could provide her company with repertory. Although Rambert had choreographed her own dances as a soloist, her great gift was to recognize and cultivate talent in others. Her prodding of Ashton and Fedorovitch led them to embark on careers from which de Valois would later profit: indeed, with Ashton, the Vic-Wells company acquired its most important choreographer. De Valois has a vivid memory of attending a performance of his first ballet, *A Tragedy of Fashion*, and going backstage to congratulate Rambert on finding "a real choreographer."[35]

The carefully planned strategy that enabled de Valois to bring Ashton to Sadler's Wells on a full-time basis in 1935 was a boon for the young company, as it was for Ashton: for all her genius, Rambert could never offer him the security of a regular salary and the backing of a fully professional organization that de Valois could. Privately, Rambert must have found it galling that her discoveries, especially in the early years, often ended up at the Wells. Until the beginning of the Second World War, however, the two companies often shared personnel: Alicia Markova as well as the young Margot Fonteyn were among the dancers who shuttled back and forth, "appear[ing] at the Mercury in the weekend performances and on their free nights from the Wells."[36] Ashton, too, returned on occasion to choreograph for Rambert, despite his expanding activities at Sadler's Wells.

De Valois saw the two companies as related but different animals. She considered them both a part of the repertory theater movement, linked in style and atmosphere to the repertory theaters that had played such an important role in her development. "Everybody loved the Mercury Theatre," she wrote in a 1975 "tribute" to the theater:

> In spite of its smallness, its atmosphere for me was not far removed from that of the Festival Theatre, Cambridge, and the Abbey Theatre, Dublin. There was dedication; there was the love of the development of the theatre for itself; there was always a stream of dancers, actors and actresses ready to offer their services.
>
> On the part of Dame Marie Rambert there was a devoted service given to the young artists that came her way, and Ashley Dukes—a distinguished author and critic—saw that his little theatre served the young actors, actresses and dramatists of the day.[37]

But de Valois also felt that without a master plan such small idealistic theaters could never grow into fully professional endeavors. As she remarked in the 1970s, "I think I loved such theatres and their efforts perhaps as much as I loved developing and giving security to those who came my way from such places, and continued to serve the place they came from whenever possible."[38]

Four decades earlier, in *Invitation to the Ballet*, de Valois had linked these two loves in a discussion of the Rambert and Jooss companies, which she offered as examples of the *ballet intime*. Comparing Rambert's approach to Jooss's, she wrote:

> The Ballet Rambert...stands for the encouragement of the young dancer and choreographer in the medium of that ballet which demands a tradi-

tional classicism. Individuality and originality are not exploited at the expense of orthodox knowledge and training. This is a courageous and unusual standpoint for the *ballet intime* to take, one that cannot but be commended. The successful members of such an organisation consequently are not cut off, but actually prepared for a career, if desired, in the larger scale ballet companies. They perform every Sunday in their own club's private theatre, and constantly give seasons in the smaller West End theatres which enable their valuable work to be presented to the general public.[39]

De Valois's remarks illustrate another major social distinction between her company and Rambert's. If the Vic-Wells company, from its inception, was intended to serve a broad popular audience, Rambert's company catered to a small and relatively exclusive public. The Ballet Club was just what its name implied—a private club with members. Only members could attend Ballet Club performances, and memberships had to be purchased before the season began. The price of membership was not especially high—ten shillings for those over twenty-one, five for younger patrons. However, with individual tickets ranging from a high of 7s/6d to a low of 2s/6d, the cheapest seat at the Ballet Club was five times the price of a sixpenny seat in the gallery at Sadler's Wells or a fivepenny seat in the gallery at the Old Vic. Aristocrats and artists mingled at the Ballet Club. In fact, its membership was a veritable who's who of the English arts and patronage elite, including such figures as Anthony Asquith, Lord Berners, Oswald Birley, Arthur Bliss, Lady Bonham Carter, Charles B. Cochran, Lady Colefax, Lady Diana Cooper, Douglas Cooper, Lady Cunard, Baron Frédéric d'Erlanger, Beryl de Zoete, Lady Juliet Duff, Gabrielle Enthoven, Jacob Epstein, Edwin Evans, Viscount Hambleden, Rupert Hart-Davis, Sir William Jowitt, Geoffrey Keynes, John Maynard Keynes, Lydia Lopokova, Iain MacNab, Norman Marshall, Oliver Messell, Lord Moore, Montagu Norman, Countess of Roseberry, Viola Tree, and Geoffrey Whitworth.[40]

The subscribers set the tone for Ballet Club performances. A critic for *The Observer* referred to the "atmosphere of Versailles."[41] Adding to the tone of exclusivity was the small size of the Mercury, where the audience and performers shared a space that was not much bigger than the salons in which Rambert had danced as a young woman in Paris. Agnes de Mille, who studied with Rambert in the 1930s, described it as having "the air of a tiny eighteenth-century princeling's court theater."[42] Evening dress at premieres was common. A room for the romantic ballet prints that Rambert and Dukes collected was eventually added next to the theater, as was a bar stocked with vintage wines and presided over by Dukes. (A special midnight performance of *Bar aux Folies-Bergère* inaugurated the bar in 1934.) The surrounding neighborhood added to the "toney" atmosphere, as did the well-to-do ladies who frequented Rambert's classes. "I was with all sorts of snobbish students," recalled Antony Tudor, who had

grown up in Finsbury and found that his working-class accent and "unfa-
miliarity with the fashionable world" caused him to be "excluded from
their parties," although he was "far too busy to waste time resenting such
slights."[43]

This is not to say that Rambert set out to exclude the general public
from the Ballet Club's Thursday and Sunday-night performances. However, with the Mercury occupied on other nights by her husband's theater
company, the only way to circumvent the law prohibiting performances
on the Sabbath was to present her group under the aegis of a private club,
as a private rather than a public event—a solution, in fact, that was adopted by many English repertory companies. As soon as it was possible to do
so, Rambert rented West End theaters and offered public seasons, but
these were relatively few and far between. In time, the distinction between
the Wells as a people's theater and the Mercury as a venue for the arts elite
became solidified in the perception of audiences as well as critics. As
William Chappell once remarked: "The Ballet Club was really a very ele-
gant thing.... We used to have the most fantastic, glittering audiences."[44]
But, as time proved, neither glamour nor elegance was enough to keep the
Ballet Club growing.

Ashton gives a sense of the difference between the two companies in
an explanation of why he left the "Versailles" of Notting Hill Gate:

> I was a little against the Ballet Club when it started. I begged Rambert to
> be more active in the professional theatre because I found the club con-
> stricting and I longed to get away. I wanted a wider field and a bigger
> stage. That was where Ninette was sensible. She got a proper theatre,
> instead of occasional performances with a piano. One wanted more than
> that.
>
> It was totally different from the Ballet Club at the Wells. Lopokova
> used to call Ninette's little troupe "the ugly ducklings". They were all effi-
> cient, while Rambert's girls were beautiful. However, the Wells was gen-
> erally an improvement. It gave me security. It gave me a regular salary,
> which I hadn't had before, and I was immensely appreciative of the luxury
> of using proper dancers at last and having proper facilities. It was very
> stimulating working with Constant [Lambert] and Sophie Fedorovitch
> and having de Valois there and the whole thing growing and expanding
> and getting better.[45]

By 1934, the year of *Bar aux Folies-Bergère*, Rambert had known de
Valois for many years. They had taken class together at Cecchetti's studio,
pooled their companies for Camargo Society performances, and
exchanged dancers and other personnel for special projects and occasions.
Like Dukes, she was also aware of de Valois's unusual range as a choreographer.

In the decade before *Bar aux Folies-Bergère*, de Valois had explored a
variety of styles, genres, and movement idioms. *Bar* was a character ballet:
it employed pointework, was rich in character and comic incident, and

evoked a series of moods—elements that linked it to Massine's character ballets of the period.⁴⁶ True to her goal of a company offering "classical and modern ballet side by side,"⁴⁷ de Valois did not confine herself to producing one "type" of ballet.

The list of her ballets between 1926 and 1934 reveals a remarkable range of styles, from the expressionism of *Rout* and the Noh-inspired works of her Abbey period, to light, demi-caractère works.⁴⁸ Typical of the latter, *Douanes* (1932) was set in a mid-nineteenth-century French customs house, offered witty portraits of passport officers and eccentric travelers (including a tightrope walker played by de Valois herself), and ended with an English country dance. She also choreographed divertissement-style works, such as *Fête Polonaise* (1931), which had variations influenced by Petipa, a major ballerina role for Phyllis Bedells, and extensive pointework. Although Mozart (*Les Petits Riens*, 1928), Bach (*Suite de Danses*, 1930), Glinka (*Fête Polonaise*), and Tchaikovsky (*Pas de Trois Classique*, 1931) figured among her musical choices, de Valois was not afraid to tackle modern composers, including Stravinsky (*Les Trois Graces*, 1928), Ralph Vaughan Williams (*The Picnic*, 1929), and Bliss (*Narcissus and Echo*, 1932). One of her most interesting works from this period was *La Création du Monde* (1932), to the jazz-inspired score by Darius Milhaud that Jean Borlin had used nine years before in his African creation myth for the Ballets Suédois.⁴⁹ Given de Valois's insistence on the close integration of music and movement, her version of the ballet must have been, like *Rout*, an intriguing choreographic study of the interrelationship of modern movement and modern music. In fact, *Création* was very much influenced by the movement style of *Rout*.⁵⁰

De Valois's most important work prior to *Bar aux Folies-Bergère* was *Job*, choreographed for the Camargo Society. Like *Création*, *Job* stands at the other end of the stylistic spectrum from *Bar*, although it shares important characteristics with it, including a connection with Diaghilev. The idea for the ballet originated with Geoffrey Keynes, the economist's brother and an authority on William Blake, who found in the latter's engravings of the Biblical story "innumerable suggestions...for attitudes and groupings, which cried out for their conversion by a choreographer into actuality and movement." He prepared a detailed scenario and asked his sister-in-law, the artist Gwendolyn Raverat, to design the backdrops for the production as well as make a series of maquettes with cutouts indicating the placement of the characters at climactic points in the action. Keynes persuaded Ralph Vaughan Williams to write the score and in 1927 sent the scenario to Diaghilev with great hopes, only to have it rejected as "too English."⁵¹ When the Camargo Society was formed, Keynes approached de Valois about doing the ballet and showed her the models. The composer agreed to the project with the proviso that she change the title of the ballet to "A Masque for Dancing" (his title for the music) and eliminate pointework from the choreography. "He needn't have worried," she later said. "I had no intention of using it."⁵²

The resulting work drew heavily on the multiple modern dance vocabularies that de Valois had been developing since the mid-1920s. The movement was powerful, austere, and plastic, with a highly effective use of counterpoint in the juxtaposition of still and moving groups. The stage was multileveled, as at the Festival Theatre. The Godhead (Job's spiritual self) sat on a throne at the head of a flight of broad steps where his winged Children moved, while the mortals were confined to the stage below. The dancers were barefoot. This, like the Central European influence that, in Cyril W. Beaumont's view, "cause[d] the angular and jerky elements of movement to be overstressed,"[53] prompted considerable criticism of the work and a spirited rejoinder from de Valois that was published in *The Dancing Times*. "I often hear [*Job*] accused of not being a ballet. Let those dance critics try to cast it with anything but really skilled dancers. A production requiring such dancers *is* a ballet, although it may not use one movement of an everyday class lesson!"[54]

Although the vocabulary and theme of *Job* differed vastly from those of *Bar aux Folies-Bergère*, both works were grounded in outside visual sources—Blake in the case of *Job* and Manet in that of *Bar*. As would occur in *Bar* with respect to the Manet painting, many of the poses in *Job* were inspired by Blake's engravings. De Valois did not precisely "copy" the poses of Blake's figures. Rather, in the way of all creative artists, she selected what was useful for her. Sometimes she imitated the images quite closely, but more often she used them as a repertory of visual ideas to

William Blake, "The Just Upright Man is laughed to scorn," illustration for the Book of Job, 1823-1826. Line engraving.

draw on, transform, combine, and modify. She would use these techniques again in later works, most notably in two of her major ballets to follow *Bar*—*The Rake's Progress* (1935), based on William Hogarth's series of paintings, and *The Prospect Before Us* (1940), based on the satirical drawings of Thomas Rowlandson.

Job was the last major work of de Valois's early years as a choreographer, a summing-up of all that had come before. Unfortunately, her notes for the ballet have not survived. However, by examining the notebook for *Bar aux Folies-Bergère*, especially in light of her writings of the early 1930s, one gains considerable insight into her choreographic strategies of the period. Like *Job*, *Bar* was inspired by an art work in a medium other than ballet; like *Job*, too, it was based on a theme suggested to de Valois, rather than conceived by her. But, in each case, she made the material her own, treating it in a way that was representative of the working methods she had evolved since the mid-1920s.

Scene from the 1948 Sadler's Wells production of Job, *with new designs by John Piper.*

Bar aux Folies-Bergère

In her autobiography, *Quicksilver*, Marie Rambert recalls that it was her husband, Ashley Dukes, who came up with the idea of a ballet based on Manet's last major painting. "We had in the company," she wrote, "a very young dancer who strikingly resembled the barmaid in Manet's *Bar aux Folies-Bergère*. Her name was Elisabeth Schooling. Ashley used to chuck her under the chin whenever he passed her and say, 'There goes Manet's "Fille au Bar."'"[1] An author, dramatist, producer, and theater critic who had lived for a time in Paris and translated French plays, Dukes was an ardent Francophile.[2] He must have first seen Manet's painting at the home of his friend, the great art collector Samuel Courtauld, who acquired it in 1926 and hung it in the restored eighteenth-century dining room. Rambert loved the picture as well. Angus Morrison remembers her enthusing about it one evening after dining with the Courtaulds in Portman Square. "Ooh, my dear, to eat in that dining room with such a beautiful painting!"[3]

Dukes not only conceived the subject of the ballet, but also wrote the scenario. Initially, he offered it to Frederick Ashton, who two years before had choreographed *Foyer de Danse*, a work inspired by Degas, for Rambert's Ballet Club. Not wanting to repeat the formula so soon after *Foyer*, Ashton declined the offer. Dukes then approached de Valois with the idea "one evening over dinner at Campden Hill," where the couple lived.[4] De Valois was intrigued. Shortly after, Dukes sent her a letter outlining the scenario. He had done careful research on Paris night life of the 1880s and 1890s and knew all about the famous dancers—La Goulue, Nini Patte en l'air, Hirondelle, Grille d'Egout, La Môme Fromage—who had appeared at the Folies-Bergère and other popular venues. Now they reappeared in his scenario, along with six fictional characters. "He wrote out all the action with all the characters," recalls Dame Ninette, "ending the letter, 'Here it is, for what it's worth. Do what you will with it.'"[5]

By acting on Dukes's idea, de Valois was being true to form. She herself did not always invent the subjects of her ballets; she was often content to work from scenarios devised by others, bringing someone else's ideas to choreographic life rather than her own. She had developed the habit from girlhood, finding it a practical way of operating within the limitations of a career that had required her initially to adapt to the demands of the music hall and later to those of the repertory theater. The practice carried over to her independent creations: as we have seen, *Job* had a scenario by Geoffrey Keynes that had been originally submitted to Diaghilev, while *Rout* was choreographed to a poem that had been translated and, in all likelihood, brought to her attention by Dukes. This is not to say that de Valois lacked either the imagination or the ability to fashion her own subjects. However, in her approach to ballet-making, she was closer to an eighteenth-century artist than a nineteenth-century one, responding to the needs of occasion, audience, and patron, rather than subscribing to a romantic notion of originality. Dukes and Rambert had offered her an opportunity: she took it.

She soon became engrossed in both the scenario and the painting. "I was fascinated by all of the characters," she remembers.[6] They certainly must have resonated with her youthful experiences on the music hall stage, where she had appeared with performers not so far removed from those of the old Folies-Bergère and in surroundings that had more than a whiff of the erotic atmosphere of Manet's painting. Although these recollections certainly added to the appeal of the subject, her preparations for staging the ballet offered a demonstration of the method that she had been elaborating since the late 1920s.

Only a year before de Valois set to work on "Ashley's ballet," as they came to call it,[7] she laid this method out in the five-part series published in *The Dancing Times* under the title of "Modern Choregraphy."[8] As was befitting of the daughter of a military officer, she outlined a precise and thoroughly planned operation, a model that drew heavily on her experiences in the Diaghilev company and in the repertory theater movement. She began the third article with a list. "The production of ballet," she asserted, "must be created by the choreographer in relation to the following":

1. Music.
2. Theatrical presentation.
3. Decor and costume.
4. The dancers.

"I have put these principles in the above order," she explained, "not because I wish to declaim which is of the greatest importance, but practical experience is inclined to force the issue to be generally evolved in the above train of thought."[9] In this chapter, with the aid of the *Bar aux Folies-Bergère* notebook and the articles from the "Modern Choregraphy" series, we will follow her "train of thought" from the conception of the ballet through its realization, while comparing its "method" to other works choreographed by de Valois in the same period.

As indicated by the list, once a ballet's theme was decided upon, music became her first priority. De Valois did not personally choose the music for *Bar aux Folies-Bergère*, but following an established practice, consulted an outside musical advisor. Previously, this role had been filled by the music critic Edwin Evans, who had compiled a list of scores and recordings suitable for dance for the small library at the Academy of Choregraphic Art. She had complete faith in his judgment. A strong supporter of the Ballets Russes, he had been close to Diaghilev and was an ardent champion of Stravinsky. This time, however, de Valois turned to a friend of Evans, the young English composer and conductor Constant Lambert. He, too, had been associated with Diaghilev, who commissioned from him the score for Nijinska's 1926 ballet *Romeo and Juliet* (in which de Valois had danced the role of the Nurse during one of her guest appearances with the Ballets Russes). In 1928, de Valois had Lambert arrange the Mozart music for her first ballet at the Old Vic—*Les Petits Riens*. He soon became one of her most trusted collaborators. As her company's resident conductor and musical director, he played a key role in shaping the Vic-Wells repertory. "He was the greatest conductor and advisor that this country has had," de Valois wrote after his death in 1951. "Even today he is irreplaceable in the ballet: there is no one to equal him in that all-round knowledge and intellectual understanding demanded of this eclectic side of the theatre world."[10]

For *Bar aux Folies-Bergère*, Lambert chose seven of Emmanuel Chabrier's ten *Pièces pittoresques* for piano.[11] Lambert had great admiration for the French composer, and in *Music Ho!*, which was published within months of the ballet's premiere, he spoke of the qualities that he found so appealing:

> It is impossible to praise too highly the wit, charm and skill of this composer, whose works are still airily dismissed with the label 'light music'.... As an harmonic innovator, his influence, though acting within a smaller range is no less far reaching than that of Glinka himself.... He is, too, the only composer to have equally influenced both generations of modern French music—the pre-war aesthetic period and the post-war "tough" period.
>
> Above all, Chabrier holds one's affection as the most genuinely French of all composers, the only writer to give us in music the genial rich humanity, the inspired commonplace, the sunlit solidity of the French genius that finds its greatest expression in the paintings of Manet and Renoir.... He was the first important composer since Mozart to show that seriousness is not the same as solemnity, that profundity is not dependent upon length, that wit is not always the same as buffoonery, and that frivolity and beauty are not necessarily enemies.[12]

Even more important for de Valois's purposes, Lambert emphasized the artistic affinity between the composer and Manet, who were in fact close friends. A music lover, Manet had done two portraits of Chabrier and painted him among the revelers in "Masked Ball at the Opera." The composer often played at Manet's weekly soirées and had composed an Impromtu dedicated to the painter's wife, Suzanne, herself an accomplished pianist. For a time both artists had studios on the same street. After Manet's death in 1883 (he died in the composer's arms), Chabrier bought several important paintings at the Manet Studio Sale, including "A Bar at the Folies-Bergère," which hung over his piano for the last ten years of his life.[13] Not only did the works of Chabrier and Manet have much in common in terms of their sensibility, but, as Lambert noted, they also revealed a similar fascination with popular entertainment:

> In the heyday of the music-hall aesthetic it was often urged that since painters like Manet could produce their best work in such paintings as the Bon Bock or the Bar at the Folies Bergère, etc., there was no reason why composers should not achieve work of a similar greatness taking their inspiration from similar scenes.... After listening to the abundant gaiety of Chabrier's music, which flows forth with all the natural ease of his period, Cocteau's post-war exhortations to the younger French school to rid themselves of pomposity, to be... Gallic and gay, and to draw inspiration from the bal-musette and the street band, read painfully like one of Doctor Crane's once famous "Tonic Talks".[14]

In linking the work of these two artists and in drawing inspiration from a pictorial source, Lambert and de Valois were partly following a path laid out by Diaghilev. A passionate art lover with an encyclopedic knowledge of painting, Diaghilev frequently conceived ballets at least partly in terms of their visual style. Thus, *L'Après-midi d'un Faune* was indebted to Greek archaic and classical art; *Legend of Joseph*, to the mannerist visions of Paolo Veronese; and *Parade*, to cubism. In certain ballets, such as *Carnaval*, which had music by Robert Schumann and costumes in Biedermeier style, design was used to interpret a period theme largely established by the music. In still other ballets, the visual source was directly invoked: the costumes for *Las Meninas*, for example, were copies of the dresses in Velázquez's masterpiece.

Diaghilev, however, never made a painting "come to life" as literally as de Valois and Chappell did in *Bar aux Folies-Bergère*. The device was used, however, in Jean Borlin's *El Greco* (1920), a series of tableaux vivants—or "mimed scenes"—inspired by several paintings by El Greco, including his celebrated "View of Toledo," which was reproduced as the backdrop.[15] Tableaux vivants, modeled on famous paintings or sculptures were common in popular theater in the late nineteenth and early twentieth century and at private gatherings, especially among the upper classes in the form of often quite elaborate and carefully rehearsed party entertainments.

Lambert and de Valois may well have discovered Chabrier in the musical interludes that frequently accompanied Diaghilev's performances in London: indeed, the composer's "Menuet pompeux," one of the *Pièces pittoresques* featured in the score for *Bar aux Folies-Bergère*, was often played in the postwar period, when these interludes became commonplace. Another link between *Bar* and the postwar Ballets Russes repertory was *La Boutique Fantasque*, Massine's enormously popular ballet with a bubbly cancan for Lopokova that always brought down the house. A cancan also appeared in *Bar*, led now by Alicia Markova in the role of La Goulue, the ballet's "*étoile du Can-Can*." Doubtless, there were many in the Mercury audience who were remembering—and silently comparing—

her version of the spirited dance with its Ballets Russes predecessor.

Once the music was chosen, the task that presented itself to the choreographer was twofold. In the second of her "Modern Choreography" articles, de Valois explained what this task entailed. "There are two things a young choreographer of to-day should try and develop," she wrote, "a sense of the mood and period of the music, and a knowledge of its pattern."[16]

It is on the latter point that de Valois is most insistent and expansive. She writes with a sense of excitement and discovery, and with the urgency of someone with a message to convey. That message—that the close analysis of musical form integrated with the dancer's movement is the cornerstone of a successful ballet—inevitably links her practice as a choreographer with the new developments in twentieth-century dance music promoted by Diaghilev. In the ballet world of her youth, she notes, all a choreographer needed was a sense of "the mood and period.... Melody was predominate in early ballet composition, the phrasing and time signatures of a simple form."[17] Modern scores, however, demand a more thorough musical knowledge on the part of the choreographer, as well as a knowledge of the integration of music and movement that could be learned through the study of eurhythmics. This knowledge de Valois claimed for herself, although not to the degree she would have liked. She knew enough about the piano to accompany her mother when she sang for parties of relatives and friends.[18] And she had studied eurhythmics at Mrs. Wordsworth's school. Although she characterized her training as "only the simplest tuition," she came away "know[ing] enough in theory about a printed piece of music to go up to the piano and unravel technically something I cannot altogether trust my ear to do for me. I have found even this slight knowledge invaluable when composing ballets to difficult modern music."[19]

The notebook was a fundamental part of de Valois's strategy for integrating music and movement. "On the page in my note book facing the one with my choregraphic notes," she explained to readers of *The Dancing Times*,

> I write my corresponding music notes. The pattern of the two coincide.
> The printed music is marked off in the same way, so a sudden change of
> pianist does not give any trouble. I find this method forms a framework
> that time does not easily shatter, or quick production and insufficient
> rehearsal leave little but chaos when it comes to a revival with many
> changes in the cast. Further it is a "fool-proof" method of dealing with
> difficult modern music, and the fact that not every member of the corps de
> ballet has a highly developed musical ear.[20]

De Valois got the idea of using a notebook—as well as the idea of notating the musical score—from Massine and Nijinska. De Valois remembers Massine drawing her over during a rehearsal and showing her the notebook in which he had plotted the choreography and matched it to the musical accompaniment. "I was only a dancer then," she reminisced in 1985, "but he knew I was terribly interested in all aspects of creating a ballet, and he may have had a sense that this would be useful to me some-day: in fact, he told me that himself."[21] She also remembers that Nijinska, when choreographing *Les Noces*, worked directly from a score "with the ballet worked out on it," and that the dancers rehearsed with a pianola.[22]

De Valois insisted that the relationship between music and movement had to be thoroughly assimilated by the dancers and integrated into their concept of the ballet. Her discussion of this issue is one of the most inter-esting and thoroughly considered in the "Modern Choregraphy" articles. The passage that follows makes clear the importance she attaches to music and her understanding of the problems faced by dancers who must deal with a complex musical score they may not be able to read and cannot consult in performance:

> [I]t is absolutely essential to make a corps de ballet regard themselves as another orchestra, and to give them, at the start, a *mental* picture of their music, and allow their own intelligence to develop the *oral* appreciation gradually at later rehearsals.
>
> Therefore a system of counting should be worked out according to the "phrasing" of the music. Lack of melody, odd bars, frequent changes of time signatures, are all common pitfalls of modern composition, and the dancer has not the music in front of him to refresh his memory. Counting to a steady time signature is not always advisable, because it is often just a time signature and bears no relation to the actual pattern of the musical phrase, which may start on the last beat of one bar and end on the first of another.
>
> Of course this system can be very abused through ignorance, lack of a natural musical sense, or simplest knowledge of musical technicalities. But I do not force such methods on my company blindly. Unless unduly hard pressed, I show them what is happening and why the "counting" must vary in places. They know how many bars are allotted to each chore-graphic movement, and what they are counting to each bar.[23]

De Valois was also concerned about the difference between the score as heard in rehearsal in a piano reduction and as played by a full orchestra in performance. She writes of devoting an entire rehearsal to helping the dancers cope with the difficulties of the orchestral version, in which

> [c]ounter movements are often introduced into a score, melodies non-existent in the piano [version]. The dominant piano melody in the full orchestral version may have become entirely subordinate to another. It is always advisable, if working on a piece with two distinct movements, to go over the score with your conductor and find out what will eventually predominate.[24]

This, of course, was not a problem in *Bar aux Folies-Bergère*, as the original music was written for piano. But even here, the danced version of the score differed in several notable ways from the concert form of the individual pieces. Although a few were played straight through (notably, "Mélancolie" and "Tourbillon"), most were subtly altered by Lambert to meet the needs of the action. Some of these adjustments involved cuts (a small one in "Idylle"; more extensive ones in "Scherzo-valse" and "Danse villageoise" (which was played as an overture) and the elimination of repeats. Others involved changes in tempo (slower than normal in "Tourbillon" and faster than usual in "Idylle"). In one case ("Mauresque") the last five bars were transposed a fourth higher into D Major to smooth the transition to the "Menuet pompeux" that followed.[25] The score that emerged fit the action like a glove, while remaining faithful to the music written by Chabrier.

Dancers must not only count, de Valois insisted. They also had to listen to the score so as to absorb its musical subtleties. "I know too well," she wrote,

> how irritating it is to hear a dancer counting blindly, ignorant of the form of the work, and making no effort to listen to the music. Only by listening can the light and shade of music penetrate, and tone is as much a part of the ultimate musical picture as the phrasing and technical points one analyses at the beginning.[26]

De Valois's musical views—especially her insistence on the need for an in-depth analysis of the score both on the part of the choreographer and the dancer—must have been a source of contention in the English dance community, given that she feels compelled to defend them. She does so with her usual spirit and eloquence:

> It has been said that these views lead to a mechanical effect, killing the spirit of the music, etc. But this is not a very sound argument. Analysis kills the spirit where the abilities are limited, and bores those who lack interest, concentration and discipline. Artists who aim at real efficiency are able to survive any work in detail, and enjoy the spirit of it all afterwards.[27]

From music de Valois passes to theatrical presentation, the subject of the fourth article of her series. The success or failure of a ballet, she asserts, lies solely in how its theme is presented. "No ballet should be condemned for its lack of subject matter, or because it is overburdened with the same. It is a question of treatment, whether in the former case the mood or symbolic meaning contains a mental stimulus of any value, or whether in the latter case the subject matter is an emotional one moving forward with sufficient force and clarity."[28] Crucial to such treatment is the choreographer's knowledge of "theatrical presentation." The choreographer must be concerned not only with the steps but also with how they are presented within the context of the modern theater: lighting and scenery must receive the same care as choreography. From the "ballet room to the playhouse, from the scene dock to the switch-board should his feeling and imagination take him."[29]

Like Terence Gray in his productions at the Festival Theatre, de Valois laid great stress on the importance of lighting. It was something, she wrote, that "should always be in the mind of the producer. If his thoughts continually centre round this matter, it is easy to give an impression of harmony when he has to enlist the help of a lighting technician."[30] Equally important—and another measure of her debt to the repertory theater movement—was her concern for the overall "rhythm" of a production, the "join," as she put it, between dances, scenes, and "light plots":

> I call special rehearsals to study the harmony between dances—there must be an invisible link, if necessary one dance actually intruding on the music of another—and this can be done after the arrangement of the dances. It is the point where choreography has to meet production on an absolutely even footing. It is the rhythm of ballet production. A ballet which relies for a round of applause to break the atmosphere for the next movement (as in perfectly straight-forward divertissement) is theatrically wrong. It is a mistake every choreographer makes from time to time, and I can attribute some personal failures to this very fault.[31]

For de Valois a ballet was more than its dances or "interior" details: it had to have an overall shape—a beginning, middle, and end—worked out early in the planning stages, before the actual choreography was underway. "In the study of the theatrical presentation of a ballet," she wrote, "whether period or modern, the principle [sic] stage pictures, the pictorial mood of the opening and finish, together with the all-important central point, should be decided upon after a few days familiarity with the music."[32] For the opening and closing sections of *Bar aux Folies-Bergère*, she took her cue from the dreamy, melancholic atmosphere of Manet's picture and from the barmaid who stands at its center. It is with her that we identify, and it is her world that forms the essential subject of the ballet. She is the focus of the work's first and final moments: we see her setting the bar in order and closing it for the night—the routines of a dreary, dead-end life. Set to Chabrier's evocative "Mélancolie," these sections create a musical, dramatic, and choreographic "parenthesis" around the high-spirited dancing at the ballet's center. Unifying and balancing the work, they also establish its underlying bittersweet mood.

Three years after the premiere of *Bar*, Cyril W. Beaumont published a detailed description of the action in his *Complete Book of Ballets*. His synopsis, the only complete account by an eyewitness, is worth quoting in full:

> When the curtain rises, the barmaid is seen standing behind the counter, gazing vacantly into space. Recalling herself with an effort, she finds occupation in dusting the bottles, polishing the glasses, and arranging her hair.
>
> Enter Adolphe and Gustave, two frequenters of the bar, who already seem to see things through a haze. They subside into chairs by the counter and order drinks.

Edouard Manet, "A Bar at the Folies-Bergère," 1881-1882. Oil on canvas.
Courtauld Institute Galleries, London.

Valentin the waiter bustles in. He is succeeded by Grille d'Egout who, after a spirited display of high spirits, seats herself at one of the small tables. Valentin serves her with a drink, steals a kiss, pats her knee, and strokes her arms—all in a twinkling. The other Can-Can girls come in and are soon busy exchanging confidences. The two friends at the bar begin telling each other interminable stories of their successes as anglers.

Meanwhile, Valentin has transferred his attentions to the barmaid. At his entreaty she leaves the counter and dances with him. It is plain that she is in love with the handsome waiter.

A gay old gentleman arrives on the scene and, seeing the girls, chucks them under the chin. They go out and return with La Goulue, the star of the Folies-Bergère. The old gentleman, excited by all this beauty, claps his hands and offers to stand champagne all round. For his benefit the girls dance a spirited Can-Can, which meets with his cordial approval.

Now La Goulue renders a solo. The susceptible Valentin, carried away by her flashing eyes, mincing steps, and frothy petticoats, forsakes the barmaid for the star.

Gradually the dancers and habitués take their departure until there remain only Adolphe, Gustave, and the barmaid. A slatternly woman comes in with a pail and floor-cloth. Seeing the two men dozing by the counter, she throws a little water on them. They awake with a start, place each a visiting-card on the counter, and, staggering to their feet, go off arm-in-arm.

Pearl Argyle in the opening poses of Bar aux Folies-Bergère, *1934. Photo by Pollard Crowther. Rambert Dance Company Archives.*

The barmaid slowly tears up the cards, places her elbows on the counter, and, resting her chin on her knuckles, stares fixedly into space.[33]

* * *

Just as de Valois paid close attention to the logical development of the action, so, like Diaghilev, she was concerned with fusing all the ballet's visual elements. "I am entirely against settings and costumes being the work of two separate artists," she asserted in the fourth article of the "Modern Choregraphy" series. "They should be related, and appear incomplete when viewed apart."[34] In keeping with this Diaghilev "lesson," she commissioned the sets and costumes for *Bar aux Folies-Bergère* from William Chappell. Chappell loved French impressionist and post-impressionist painting, and "knew [Manet's] picture well." Like de Valois, he first saw it at the Courtaulds, where Lydia Lopokova had taken him one day to tea, an awesome experience, he later recalled, that made him feel "very young." Chappell had originally trained to be a visual artist, only to be "conscripted"—or "hijacked"—into Rambert's company, after attending a class at her studio. Rambert needed more men, and with her characteristic enthusiasm prodded him to continue dancing, which he did.[35] In *Bar aux Folies-Bergère* (where he played Adolphe, one of the habitués), as in many other Rambert productions, Chappell served a dual role, dancing as well as designing the sets and costumes.

Like the other collaborators, Chappell did a considerable amount of

Henri Toulouse-Lautrec, "Divan Japonais," 1892–1893. Poster, color lithograph.

(RIGHT) Bar aux Folies-Bergère: *Alicia Markova as La Goulue and Frederick Ashton as Valentin, 1934. Rambert Dance Company Archives.*

research to evoke the atmosphere of the Folies-Bergère as seen through Manet's eyes. "I took everything I could out of Manet's paintings," he later said, "and when I couldn't find a prototype went elsewhere."[36] He studied posters of the period as well as fashion plates and costume books. As La Goulue, Markova wore a hat and dress inspired by the dancer Jane Avril in the famous Toulouse-Lautrec poster "Divan Japonais." "You know, [Avril] was so thin; I thought she rather looked like Alice [sic]."[37] As the waiter Valentin, Ashton wore a long white apron that could easily have come from another Manet painting, "Chez le père Lathuille." Indeed, in one of the ballet's production photographs, he stands with a napkin under his arm, much like the waiter in the picture. The top-hatted Gustave, one of the bar's "habitués," and Le Vieux Marcheur (or "old gent," as Rambert calls him in the notebook) could have stepped out of any number of Manet paintings, including "Musique aux Tuileries" at London's National Gallery. As Adolphe, the ballet's other "habitué," Chappell wore an ocher jacket, flowing black tie, and "little squashed hat" that bore a striking resemblance to Manet's own dress in his "Self-Portrait with a Palette." Intending to garb himself as an artist, Chappell confessed that he "probably did pinch" the outfit from Manet's painting.[38] The result was a "very passable" evocation of place and period, a remarkable achievement considering the minuscule budget. "I was not allowed the kind of material I liked. I had to do with net and spotted muslin. For [Mary] Skeaping's costume [as Nini Patte en l'air, one of the four grisettes] I was allowed cheap satin and a bit more for Markova, but of course one only had tuppence to spend."[39]

As Chappell himself has pointed out, neither the set nor the costume for the barmaid was an exact rendering of Manet's original. "I couldn't paint the mirrored reflection of the man in the painting, and of course one had to modify the outfits so that the dancers could dance in them."[40] For

(RIGHT) *Edouard Manet, "Self-Portrait with a Palette,"*
1878-1879. Oil on canvas. Private collection, New York.
Reproduced from Sandra Orienti, The Complete Paintings of Manet
(New York: Abrams, 1967), pl. 58.

(BELOW) Bar aux Folies-Bergère: *Adolphe (center) stands*
on a chair watching La Goulue (Sally Gilmour), late
1940s. Photo by Walter Stringer. Rambert Dance Company
Archives.

the lower part of the barmaid's costume, Chappell devised a short skirt and striped stockings that he may have seen in photographs of the period. Markova was all in net—black, mauve, purple: it was "cheap," but "looked nice." Skeaping wore a white skirt with an olive green bustle. "We needed to capture the essence of the thing. I, of course, had to find my own props. We probably got the extras from some grand friend of Rambert. One was always looking for things like that from her friends, her grand friends."[41]

In addition to conferring about the details of costuming and scenery, de Valois and Chappell probably also conferred about the ballet's overall "look." Certainly, this was the ideal espoused in her "Modern Choregraphy" articles:

> when discussing the mounting of a ballet with the scene and costume designer, it is wise to make him visualise the dancers as representing so many "tones." Quite unconsciously I think most choreographers form in their minds that certain groups and scenes are meant to convey a half or full tone. One's imagination sees some particular group sombre or bright, and the movements take on a similar form.[42]

By the time de Valois entered the rehearsal studio, then, she had the entire ballet pretty much mapped out in her head, with the notebook serving as a guide. The letter that Dukes wrote to her at the beginning of their collaboration does not survive, but her memories of it—and her response to it—indicate the thoroughness of her research and the careful thought that was given to the motivations of both character and action. She recalls that his written "portraits" of the various dancers were highly detailed and that she "tried to individualize each of them" in her choreography.[43]

Not all her research was pursued in books. Markova recalls that one day after class "Madam" took her to Soho, where they wandered up and down the streets observing the prostitutes as they plied their afternoon trade. "Watch how they walk," de Valois admonished her young star, then known for her virginal air and ethereal style. "That's the quality I want in your dancing."[44] Her efforts paid off. "You just won't know Alicia when you see her," wrote Anton Dolin's mother after seeing Markova as La Goulue. "She has developed an extraordinary sense of humour, like a singer who has suddenly given evidence of feeling in her voice. Her roguish impertinence as the coquettish star of the cancan girls is a superb piece of effrontery, which makes the audience rock with laughter. Our little Alicia is finding herself at last."[45] Cyril W. Beaumont, however, noted that Markova's interpretation was "a period impression, purged of the crudity of the original, a portrait at once piquant and harmless as a salted almond, if such a comparison be permitted. She had little to do, but she did it perfectly, with such artless naughtiness, and with so engaging an air, as to be irresistible."[46]

Dame Ninette also tried to individualize the four grisettes or quadrille dancers, who formed the ballet's chamber-sized corps. In particular, she

The original cast of Bar aux Folies-Bergère, *with (from left) Frederick Ashton (Valentin), A. Gee (standing in for Diana Gould as Grille d'Egout), Walter Gore (Gustave), Pearl Argyle (La Fille au Bar), Alicia Markova (La Goulue), William Chappell (Adolphe), Tamara Svetlova (Hirondelle), Mary Skeaping (Nini Patte en l'air), and Oliver Reynolds (Le Vieux Marcheur), 1934. Photo by Pollard Crowther. Rambert Dance Company Archives.*

singled out Diana Gould, whom she cast as Grille d'Egout, sensing in her "a real talent for comedy." Gould "had not been used in this way before," de Valois explains. "She was seen largely as a serious romantic type, but I could tell that she was a born comedienne, and developed the role accordingly."[47] The reviews attested to her success. "Of the four *grisettes*," wrote D.D. in *The Daily Telegraph*. "I was chiefly struck by Diana Gould. This statuesque dancer is a surprisingly good comedienne."[48]

Another comic role was the waiter, Valentin, "a bossy old thing," as de Valois describes him, "who ran around and fussed with everything."[49] Ashton, who doubtless added many of his own character touches, played him as an outrageous flirt—"dapper, suave, deft, lively as quicksilver."[50] His wit and humor delighted the critics. Beaumont wrote that he was "brilliant," *The Times* that he was the ballet's "presiding genius."[51] Richardson in *The Dancing Times* confessed that he was not surprised by Ashton's success, "for on more than one occasion he has proved himself to be a first rate *danseur de caractère* in roles in which there is a strong element of comedy."[52]

In the all-important role of the barmaid or "La Fille au Bar," as she was called on the program, de Valois cast Pearl Argyle. (Although Elisabeth Schooling later danced the part with great success, de Valois did not consider her experienced enough at the time for such as important role.)[53] Argyle was known for her extraordinary beauty, remarked upon by virtually everyone who saw her. However, de Valois chose not to emphasize her glamour: she saw the barmaid as a woman resigned to the disappointments of life. Her love for Valentin, revealed in their pas de deux, is destined to be unrequited: he is infatuated with La Goulue. But a broken heart is not the only reason for her sadness. When at the end she tears up the calling cards left on the counter by the now lurching "habitués," the gesture reveals a weariness with her surroundings and their easy, tawdry pleasures, including those that as a barmaid she was expected to provide.[54] Initially, Argyle wanted to end the ballet by collapsing on the bar in tears. But de Valois, intent on preserving the bittersweet mood of Manet's painting, rejected this melodramatic and sentimental gesture. "No," she told Argyle, "you must remain in the original pose. Stare into the future accepting everything."[55] Argyle followed her advice and gave an inspired performance. "She had the features of a Manet," wrote Beaumont, "and...the jaded air of a young woman who...has no illusions left."[56] "Her mimetic powers," enthused Richardson, were "beyond all expectations."[57]

The premiere took place on 15 May 1934, the first night of the Rambert season, at the Mercury Theatre. The ballet was the centerpiece of an evening that opened with Andrée Howard and Susan Salaman's *Mermaid* and closed with Ashton's *Les Masques*. The press reaction was largely favorable. *The Times* called the new ballet a "study in female sauciness to music by Chabrier":

> Manet's famous picture comes to life; its figures break out of their frames, even leaping into the auditorium, and have their entrances and exits at the centre gangway. Even the befringed barmaid, looking on impassively but seeing more than she would have you believe, is stirred at last to take a turn at the *Can-can*, and so allows Miss Pearl Argyle to demonstrate her versatility. The plumes and bodice worn by Miss Diana Gould, the ostentation of Miss Markova as the star dancer, and the presiding genius of head waiter Cedric [sic] Ashton make a gay and Gallic piece, [an] instance of successful translation from one art into another.[58]

The Daily Telegraph thought that *Bar* made "a charming addition to the...repertoire." The "choreographic treatment is intelligent and amusing. Alicia Markova, an honoured guest from the Vic-Wells dances exquisitely as the star, and Pearl Argyle is Manet's figure in the flesh....There was distinction in Frederick Ashton's performance as the waiter, and the whole production was deliciously gay."[59] Richardson, although impressed by Argyle's performance as the barmaid, felt that "in the part of La Goulue...the powers of Alicia Markova are somewhat wasted."[60] Two weeks later, *Bar* was danced at a party given at the Mercury Theatre to celebrate the fifth year of the Ballet Club, the fiftieth birthday of Ashley Dukes, and the twenty-fifth anniversary of his first play.

Later critics, who saw and wrote about *Bar aux Folies-Bergère*, have viewed it, as Dame Ninette herself does,[61] as a charming, but slight and definitely minor part of her body of works. Nonetheless, Cyril Beaumont included a lengthy description of it in his *Complete Book of Ballets*, while Fernau Hall viewed the work as bringing an entirely new kind of realism to British ballet. He also pointed out *Bar*'s importance as a "preparation" for the "superb...earthy realism" of de Valois's next major work, *The Rake's Progress* (1935), in its "fine sense of character and...mordant, satirical sense of humour." According to Hall, de Valois

> did not attempt to equal the realism of the original: the courtesans and demi-reps of Manet and Toulouse-Lautrec are made amusing but essentially respectable, and the Can-Can could scarcely raise a blush on the most maidenly cheek. Nevertheless, the dances have a brash vulgarity quite new in English ballet, and the cynical disillusion of the barmaid is presented without a trace of sentimentality. The main weakness of *Bar aux Folies-Bergère* is the excessive use of mime: the dances, starved of their quota of action, are accordingly feeble in style and excessively repetitive. The best things about the ballet are its precise economic characterisation and its racy atmosphere.[62]

Whatever its shortcomings, *Bar* was a popular addition to the Rambert repertory. In fact, the ballet was so successful that by 1940 another Rambert production with de Valois as the choreographer was underway. This was *Pippa Passes*. Inspired by Robert Browning's well-known dramatic poem, the ballet was announced in the company's February–March 1940 program. Although no designer was mentioned, the composer was identified as Stanley Bate. For reasons that probably had to do with the Second World War, the project never came to fruition.[63]

Bar aux Folies-Bergere remained in the repertory of Ballet Rambert for many years. It was televised in 1938, with Elisabeth Schooling in the role that Ashley Dukes had imagined for her, and it was taken by the company on its extended tour of Australia in 1947–1949. In 1953, the ballet was dropped from the repertory, never to return. It remains alive, however, in the memories of those who danced it and those who saw it, and in the pages of the notebook where de Valois worked out its choreography.

The *Bar aux Folies-Bergère* notebook and the materials associated with it reveal that whatever natural rivalry may have existed between Ninette de Valois and Marie Rambert, their relationship was one of genuine friendship and respect. The fact that Rambert saved the notebook at all and her telling comment on its cover—"will be valuable someday"—make this clear. But the manuscript also reveals, as Jane Pritchard has pointed out, the sharp differences between the two women in outlook and dance values. "Ninette looks at feet," Rambert liked to say. "I look at eyes. That is the difference between us."[1]

The contrast is borne out by what each of them chose to record in the ballet's "score." Nearly all of de Valois's entries describe steps and concrete actions: she tells us what the dancers did and when they did it—down to the bar and counts. Rambert's entries are few, but almost always they indicate the emotional resonance of an action: the lingering of the barmaid as she stands in front of the mirror, the rolling head of the waiter as he shows her the brand of his champagne—details that impart "flavor" to a gesture.

Looking over the score in 1985, de Valois objected to some of these details as too "music hall." For instance, she expressed strong disapproval of Rambert's note about the old gentleman "cross[ing] himself behind his top hat (with which he shields himself from the view of [Markova's] 'undies')." She also took exception to the description of Markova's walk in the "Menuet pompeux" section—"pitch body front to show off bustle." She considered the movement "frivolous" as well as vulgar, the sort of thing, as she put it, that "I could see...at the Palladium any night." One feels that for de Valois, *Bar* was a much more bittersweet and shaded work than the romp suggested by Rambert's comments, which, in some instances, recorded bits of comic business added by the dancers as the ballet evolved in performance. As de Valois ruefully observed, "you couldn't stop any of them [from] doing it."[2]

Although characterization was something that de Valois talked about with the dancers and that gave the work its special charm, her "script" seldom strays from actions and events. This is almost certainly because she used the notebook as a compositional tool to think out the ballet, rather than a means of describing the choreography once this had been set, as was the case of Rambert.

The notebook reveals with unusual clarity de Valois's working method as a choreographer. Like Massine, she devised much of the action before entering the studio: she did not require, as Ashton or Balanchine did, the physical presence of the dancers to sketch out a scene or invent a sequence of steps. "She was *tremendously* well prepared," Diana Gould recalls:

> She had tremendous, quiet authority,...[and] always looked you straight in the eye....And what she showed you...she'd rarely change, although sometimes you'd adjust something here and there. For the first time I had a real feeling of security. This was not only because of the way she choreographed, but because she was so welcoming, so nice. What I liked, above all, was her fairness and interest....You suddenly felt you were a human being and not a wretched object to be screamed at or put through its paces..., never to please.[3]

Unsurprisingly, given de Valois's interest in drama, the score is rich in mimetic detail: the grisettes "clink" their glasses, the waiter demands his money, the barmaid "tidies her hair," the "old gent" bows, kisses her hand, and "chucks" her under the chin. Nearly always, de Valois times the action precisely to the music. Nowhere is this more clearly seen than in the opening moments of the ballet: the barmaid is introduced in the pose from Manet's painting, then slowly begins to prepare the bar for the evening's activities, thus setting the stage and mood for the action to follow. In describing these preparations, de Valois indicates exactly how many beats it takes for the barmaid to "hold the picture," take up a cloth, pick up a glass, rub it on the inside, rub it on the outside, put it down, gaze in the mirror, tidy her hair, tidy her dress, take up the cloth, and wipe the counter. This close coordination of mime and music almost certainly comes from Massine, probably the single most important influence on *Bar* and de Valois's other character ballets of the period. "His character work was so wonderful," she said in 1985. "As a choreographer, he...had a basic influence on everything I've done."[4]

What the notebook does not indicate is the "room," as Diana Gould puts it, that de Valois left "for comic business" and for the expression of temperament that allowed the dancers to give individual flavor to their characterizations. Most of these nuances are probably lost forever, but they remain vivid in the memories of the performers. Gould recalls that Alicia Markova was "an absolutely natural comedienne" and that the two of them "enjoyed playing off one another." She also remembers "Freddy [Ashton] fussing around with a teeny feather duster. His job was to be frightfully fussy, fiddling around. He was awfully good, flapping away with his napkin."[5] As Gould's recollections make clear, many of these individual touches related to the comic timing and the interplay of the personalities onstage—things that are impossible to notate. The chemistry between Walter Gore and William Chappell, as the two habitués, made their performances hilarious:

> They were so good, both of them, wonderful fellows for each other. Billy [Chappell] had a kind of egg face, and Waldo [Gore] had one of the witti-

est faces I've ever known—a marvelous witty snout, an inquiring nose like a terrier. He would look at Billy, and Billy would give his sort of slightly Buster Keaton look. Oh, they were divine! They were so good![6]

De Valois remembers that audiences "loved" this bit of comic business "almost more than anything." And she recalls with delight Gould's own "marvelous" performance. "I...separated her from the other grisettes,...[who] became more like a corps group....She was the separate lady because she was so funny."[7]

Like the other grisettes as well as the old gentleman, Gould made her entrance through the audience. This device, which de Valois had initially explored at the Festival Theatre, not only heightened the sense of dramatic immediacy, but also transformed the spectators of the ballet into its active participants—made them "patrons," as it were, of the bar and its "girls." During the twelve opening bars of the "Menuet pompeux," when the grisettes moved down the aisle to the stage, Diana Gould, Sally Gilmour, and Elisabeth Schooling all remember waving and gesturing flirtatiously to members of the audience.[8] The small size of the Mercury Theatre, which seated only 157 people and had a proscenium only eighteen feet wide, made the device all the more effective.

In her treatment of the dances, de Valois tends to be less precise than in her description of the mimetic action. Like a stage director, she blocks out the choreography, highlighting what is important dramatically, and leaving the refinements for later. Thus, she says little about arms, although she is often specific about the positions—especially croisé and effacé—presenting the body to the audience. Similarly, while she frequently indicates the direction of a turn or half-turn, she seldom notes the kind of turn she wants the dancers to perform. She gives equally short shrift to traveling steps, even though she typically diagrams the direction of a cross or the shifts in floor pattern. She is very specific, however, about the themes of key dance passages. Her choreography for the barmaid in the pas de deux includes pas de basque, pas de bourrée dessous, jetés en arrière, and grands ronds de jambe en l'air en dedans; for La Goulue's solo, bourrées, walks on pointe, grands battements, arabesques à terre in plié, développés, and jetés en arrière. And, typically, when specific steps are mentioned, de Valois breaks them down musically, indicating how many bars it takes to do a succession of développés, and on exactly which count there is a backbend in a pas de basque. It is interesting to note that the step names she uses tend to be those favored by Cecchetti.

Thus, although the score is remarkably detailed, it does not record every element of the choreography in the manner of a Laban or Benesh score. The roles of the grisettes and the habitués are not differentiated, as they were in performance: the grisettes, for example, are identified in the diagrams and in the written text only by number. Moreover, the notebook is not complete. Not only are there occasional blanks, but there are also two missing sections—the "Scherzo-valse" and the reprise of "Mélancolie" that ends the ballet. Missing as well is the copy of the musical score that de Valois refers to in the notebook to clarify counts or tricky phrasing. In other words, the choreographic score that Rambert lovingly preserved cannot on its own bring the ballet back to life: human memory is needed both to fill in the gaps and add flesh to the bones of the choreography—the style that was second nature to the work's original interpreters. (As of this writing, four dancers with vivid memories of the ballet—Alicia Markova, Diana Gould, Elisabeth Schooling, and Sally Gilmour—are still alive, as is de Valois herself: thus, it may not be too late to reconstruct the ballet.)[9] Yet, even if the written record provided is only partial, the score has immense historical value, offering a remarkably intimate view of de Valois's choreographic strategies, while also revealing with an unusual richness of detail the gestures, motifs, and themes of a work that embodied a major ballet style of the 1930s.

The notebook that de Valois used was a seven-by-ten-inch "Temple Bar Loose Leaf Note Book" sold at Woolworth's. She bought the binder in 1930—the date of the calendar that appears on one of the covers—and kept it, possibly reusing it with refills that cost threepence a package. The surviving score takes up thirty-four unnumbered pages. De Valois used two pages at a time, writing across the "spine" of the book. On the extreme left she noted the timing of each sequence—first in bars, then in counts. Then, she wrote a description of the action, frequently adding diagrams to indicate changes in position and floor patterns. At the beginning of each section, she gave the title of the accompanying music and the dance counts in each bar. At the head of the "Tourbillon" section, moreover, she added a key identifying the characters in the diagrams: "O" for the barmaid; "X" for the grisettes; a square for the habitués; a cross for the waiter. She repeated the key at the start of the "Menuet pompeux" section, this time adding a black dot for the old gentleman and a diamond for the "principal grisette," Markova's role. Throughout the manuscript there are many abbreviations, and frequent inconsistencies in punctuation, capitalization, and nomenclature, and the language is often telegraphic.

In editing the transcription that follows, some of these inconsistencies have been silently eliminated. The spelling of step names has been standardized, and punctuation inserted to clarify meaning. Rambert's comments appear in italics, and editorial additions, including references to diagrams, in brackets. The bracketed page numbers correspond to the pages in the original. Otherwise, everything has been left as de Valois wrote it—and Rambert commented upon it—more than sixty years ago, when, together, they brought *Bar aux Folies-Bergère* to life.

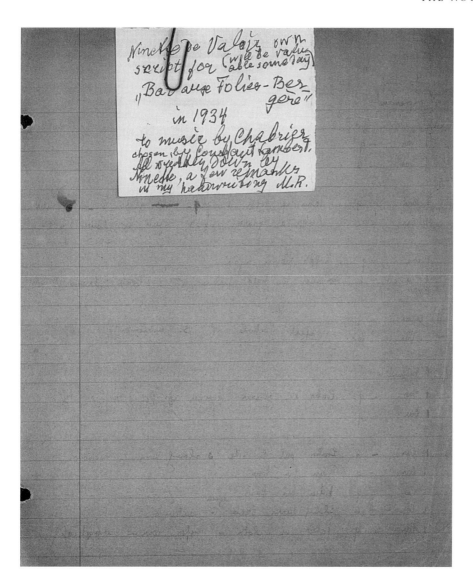

Ninette de Valois' own
script for (will be valuable someday)
"Bar aux Folies-Bergère"
in 1934
to music by Chabrier
chosen by Constant Lambert.
All written down by
Ninette, a few remarks
in my handwriting. M.R.

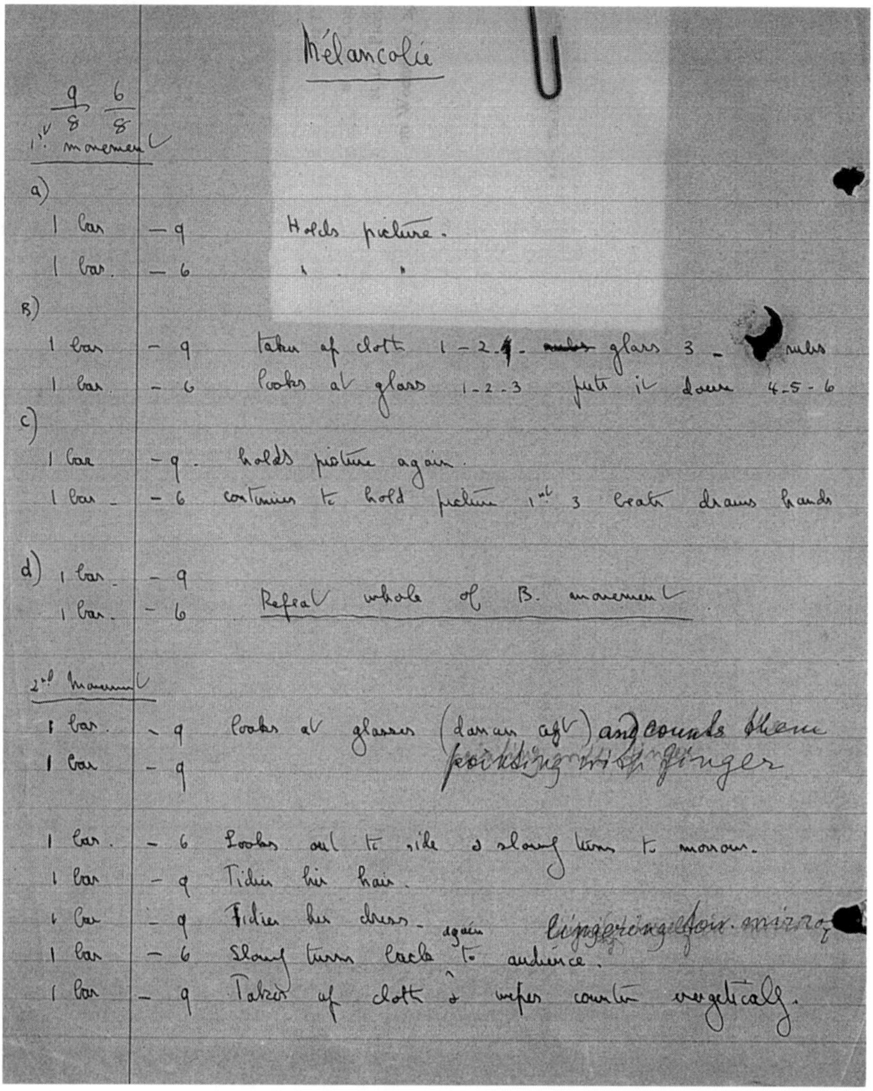

[pages 1–2]

Mélancolie

9/8 6/8

<u>1st Movement</u>

a.

1 bar	– 9	Holds picture.
1 bar	– 6	" "

b.

1 bar	– 9	Takes up cloth 1–2, glass 3; rubs glass, 4–5–6 inside—outside, 7–8–9.
1 bar	– 6	Looks at glass, 1–2–3; puts it down, 4–5–6.

c.

1 bar	– 9	Holds picture again.
1 bar	– 6	Continues to hold picture 1st 3 beats; draws hands off counter, last 3 beats.

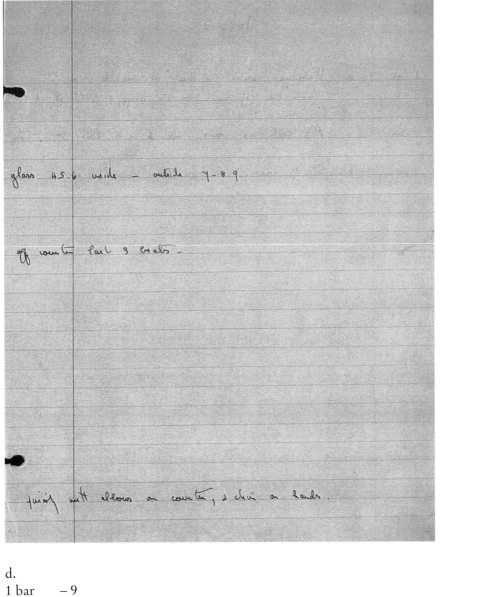

glass 45.6 inside — outside 7-8-9.

off counter last 3 beats —

finish with elbows on counter, & chin on hands.

d.

1 bar	− 9	
		<u>Repeat whole of (b) movement</u>.
1 bar	− 6	

<u>2nd Movement</u>

1 bar	− 9	Looks at glasses (dancer's left) *and counts them pointing with finger.*
1 bar	− 9	
1 bar	− 6	Looks out to side & slowly turns to mirror.
1 bar	− 9	Tidies her hair.
1 bar	− 9	Tidies her dress *lingering before mirror.*
1 bar	− 6	Slowly turns back again to audience.
1 bar	− 9	Takes up cloth & wipes counter energetically, finishing with elbows on counter & chin on hands.

[pages 3–4]

1 bar	– 6	Habitués enter & meet in middle. On the 1st beat they step out from the wings, & hold for 2 beats with leg in air—*to side*—waving their hands offstage. [DIAGRAM]
1 bar	– 9	1st 3 beats one bows, next 3 beats ditto 2nd. They raise their hats and walk upstage towards barmaid [on] last 3 beats. [DIAGRAM]
1 bar	– 6	[?] back sideways to chairs, sit down, and replace their hats. Barmaid resumes original position.

2 beats with leg in air — wag their hands — off stage.

raise their hats & walk towards Command Post 3 beats —

sit down & replace their hats. Barnard resumes original position.

[Pages 5–6]

Tourbillon

3/4		Dancers count 3 to bar.
2 bars	– 6	Waiter enters upstage, 1st bar. *Kisses barmaid's hands, lifting them over counter each in turn, holding them in both his hands.* [DIAGRAM] 2nd bar, kisses barmaid's hand.

A.

2 bars	– 6	1st grisette, 2 steps (enters upstage), stands and turns head from side to side—1 bar. <u>Repeat.</u>
2 "	– 6	Step downstage, fouetté movement with toe on ground, repeat upstage. [DIAGRAM]
2 "	– 6	Takes arm of 1st habitué, walks round—2 bars. [DIAGRAM]
2 "	– 6	Man moves forward & each turning[?] on chair. Grisette stands still. [DIAGRAM]

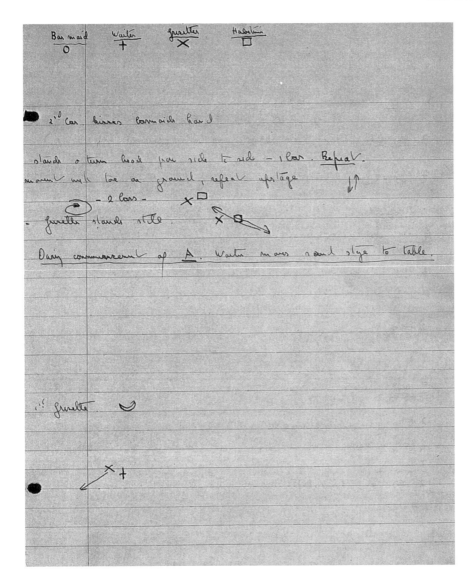

Repeat the whole of these 8 bars with 2nd habitué. During commencement of "A" waiter moves round stage to table. Finish of repeat grisette centre stage [?] on ear.

B.

8 bars — 5–6–6–7. (See music.)

5	Waiter moves across stage.
6	" " diagonally upstage to centre. [DIAGRAM]
6–7	" kisses barmaid's hands moving round 1st grisette. [DIAGRAM]

8 bars — 5–6–6–7. (See music.)

5	Waiter bows to grisette.
6	Asks her to sit down.
6	Grisette moves down to table. [DIAGRAM]
7	Waiter follows.

[Pages 7–8]

8 bars		Divided as follows:
2 bars	– 6	1st habitué claps hands & calls barmaid (standing up).
2 bars	– 6	Barmaid pours drink & hands to habitué.
		Repeat this movement with 2nd habitué for remaining 4 bars.
8 bars		Divided as follows:
2 bars	– 6	Waiter asks 1st habitué to pay. He points to the other.
2 bars	– 6	Repeat with 2nd habitué.
4 bars		Entrance of other 3 grisettes. [DIAGRAM] Position end of movement B. [DIAGRAM]
C.		
8 bars		Divided as follows:
2 bars	– 6	2nd grisette executes "splits."

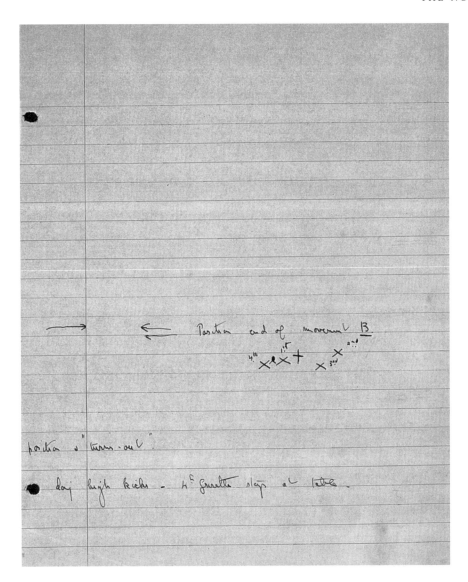

2 bars   – 6   Waiter runs behind 2nd grisette & 3rd [grisette] walks to position and "turns-out."

2 bars   – 6   Waiter runs to 3rd [grisette] and runs round holding her foot.

2 bars   – 6   3rd grisette moves diagonally upstage from table doing high kicks. 4th grisette stops at table.

[Pages 9–10]

4 bars	Divided as follows:
2 bars	1st grisette continues movement. Waiter puts 3rd grisette's foot down and runs behind 2nd to lift her up.
2 bars	They get into place for Can-Can: [DIAGRAM]

D.

8 bars		Divided as follows:
2 bars	– 6	Step "corkscrews" movement, hop into centre with high kicking movement.
2 bars	– 6	Hop back (leg held in grand battement), run round to right—one change of place. [DIAGRAMS]
		Repeat this movement for following 4 bars.
4 bars		Divided as follows:

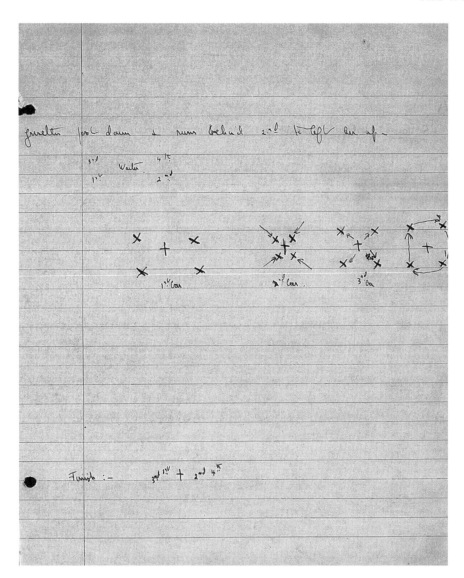

2 bars	Waiter runs downstage & sees "turn" in progress.
2 bars	" rushes round stage telling everyone.
4 bars	1st 4 beats, they hold position, closing in on 1, 2 (see music). Finish: 3rd – 1st + 2nd – 4th.

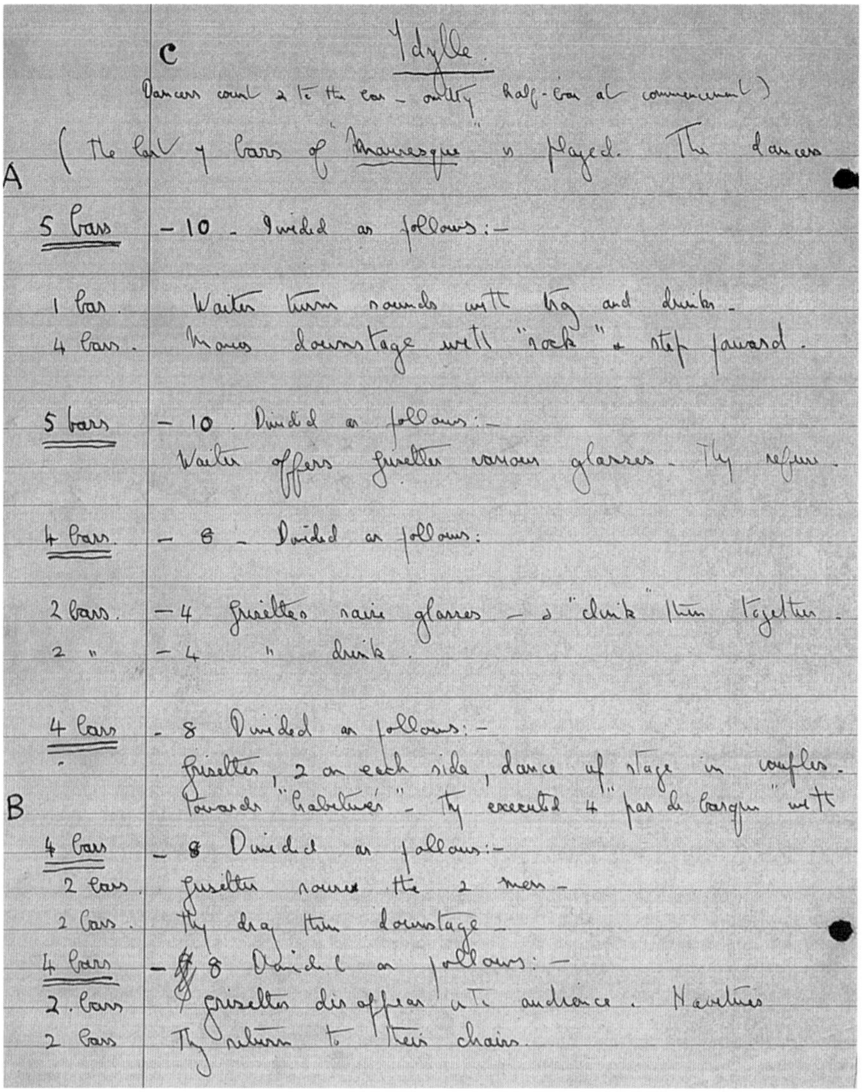

[pages 11–12]

Idylle

Dancers count 2 to the bar, omitting half-bar at commencement.
(The last 7 bars of <u>Mauresque</u> [are] played. The dancers move upstage and group
themselves round the bar.)

<u>A.</u>

<u>5 bars</u>	– 10	Divided as follows:
1 bar		Waiter turns round with tray and drinks.
4 bars		Moves downstage with "rock" & step forward executed four times. The grisettes follow him. Position at finish: [DIAGRAM]
<u>5 bars</u>	– 10	Divided as follows:
		Waiter offers grisettes various glasses. They refuse. He places tray on floor & turns his back on them.
<u>4 bars</u>	– 8	Divided as follows:

move upstge + group themselves round the bar —)

executed four times. The grisettes follow him. Position at finish

$1^{.rd} + \frac{4^{th}}{2^{.d}}$

he placed tray on floor + turns his back a them

Waiter takes tray + moves away to table.

back bend on $2^{.nd}$ beat   ↖ X X   ↑ X X

watch them.

2 bars	– 4	Grisettes raise glasses & "clink" them together. Waiter takes tray & moves away to table.
2 "	– 4	Grisettes drink.
<u>4 bars</u>	– 8	Divided as follows: Grisettes, 2 on each side, dance upstage in couples towards habitués. They execute 4 "pas de basque" with backbend on 2nd beat. [DIAGRAM]

B.

<u>4 bars</u>	– 8	Divided as follows:
2 bars		Grisettes rouse the 2 men.
2 bars		They drag them downstage.
<u>4 bars</u>	– 8	Divided as follows:
2 bars		Grisettes disappear into audience. Habitués watch them.
2 bars		They return to their chairs.

[pages 13–14]

4 bars	– 8	They move their chairs to centre & sit facing each other. 4th count, one mimes he has something to say (4).
4 bars	– 8	As follows:
2 bars		Fishes with his stick.
1 bar		Pulls "rod" out of water.
1 bar		Shows length of fish.

C.   Pas de deux.

| 4 bars | – 8 | Waiter walks astride chair, 1st bar. Sits down, 2nd bar. Repeats movement. Barmaid walks to side of bar, raises flap, and steps through. [DIAGRAM] |
| 4 bars | – 8 | Barmaid diagonally downstage as follows: [DIAGRAM] |

1 bar, pas de basque.
1 bar, turn.

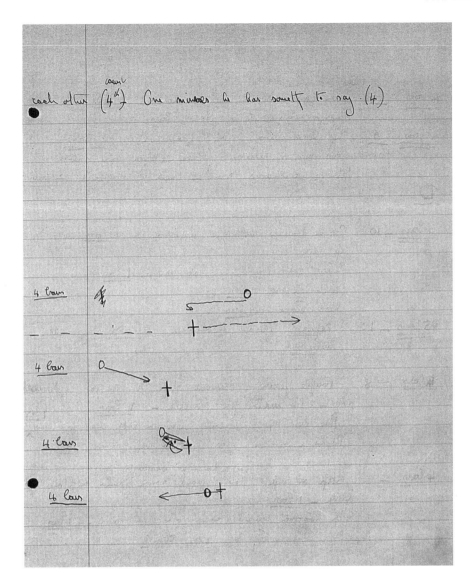

Repeat whole movement.

4 bars — 8   Takes waiter's hand & moves towards him & away [on] one side of chair (upstage), repeat downstage [on] other side of chair, turning & sitting on chair last beat. [DIAGRAM]

4 bars — 8   Step & sit back in chair—2 bars—then repeat movement twice double time. [DIAGRAM]

[pages 15–16]

4 bars	– 8	Waiter turns chair round facing audience, 2 bars. Swings chair to & fro, 2 bars. [DIAGRAM]
4 bars	– 8	They lean away from each other, 2 bars. Barmaid gets up, & waiter places chair near table. Takes barmaid's hand, back to audience, 2 bars. [DIAGRAM]

D.

5 bars	– 10	Pas de bourrée, under, in sequence for 2 bars going upstage. Jetés going round in half-circle, 1 bar. Lift across, 1 bar. Kiss twice, 1 bar. [DIAGRAMS]
5 bars	– 10	Repeat same movement downstage facing audience.
4 bars	– 8	Couple facing. Barmaid steps with r[ight] foot 4th croisé front, left with "jeté derrière," 1 bar.

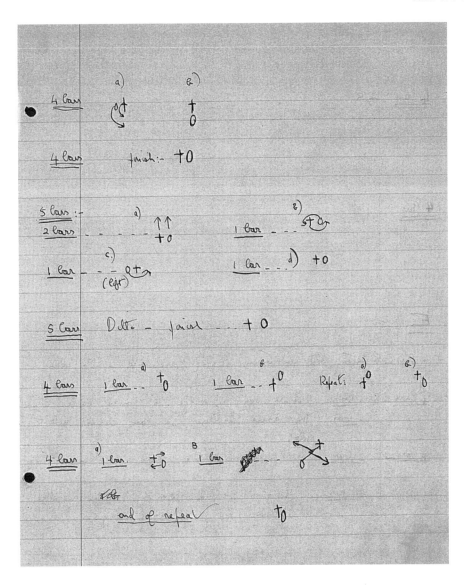

Pas de basque back, turn on both feet en dedans, <u>1 bar</u>.
<u>Repeat movement starting with other foot</u>. [DIAGRAMS]

<u>4 bars</u>   – 8   Step on right foot (hold r[ight] hand at arm length), grand rond de jambe en l'air inside, <u>1 bar</u>.
Step ~~together~~ towards each other & away, <u>1 bar</u>.
<u>Repeat completely a full circle</u>. [DIAGRAMS]
<u>End of repeat</u>.

[pages 17–18]

4 bars	– 8	
4 bars		
E.		
4 bars	– 8	Enter old gentleman through audience. The dancers see him.
4 bars	– 8	2 bars. Dancers run upstage to centre back. [DIAGRAMS]
		2 bars. They rouse habitués & carry chairs back to side. [DIAGRAM]
4 bars	– 8	2 bars. They pull habitués back to chairs. [DIAGRAM]
		2 bars. Girl goes behind counter, waiter to table. Old gentleman has just reached stage. [DIAGRAM]

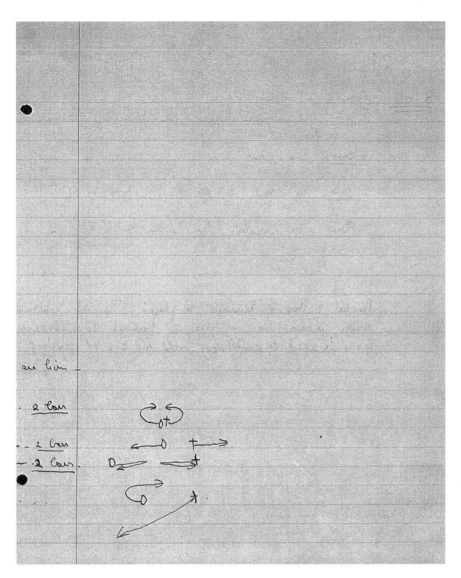

[pp. 19–20]

8 bars   Divided as follows:
2 bars. Old gentleman walks round the stage towards barmaid.
[DIAGRAM]
2 bars. He bows.
2 bars. He takes up her hand & kisses it.
2 bars. He chucks her under the chin. [DIAGRAM]
The last 7 bars of "Mauresque" [are] played. The old gentleman strolls towards table, sits down, & gazes out at audience. Waiter crosses over & talks to barmaid. *He embraces her just as the old gent. turns round to notice it. The O.G. turns his head to audience with the air of saying: have you ever seen such a thing.*

Finish :—

strolls towards table, sits down, & gazes out at audience
her just as the old gent. turns round to notice it. The O.G.
have you ever seen such a thing

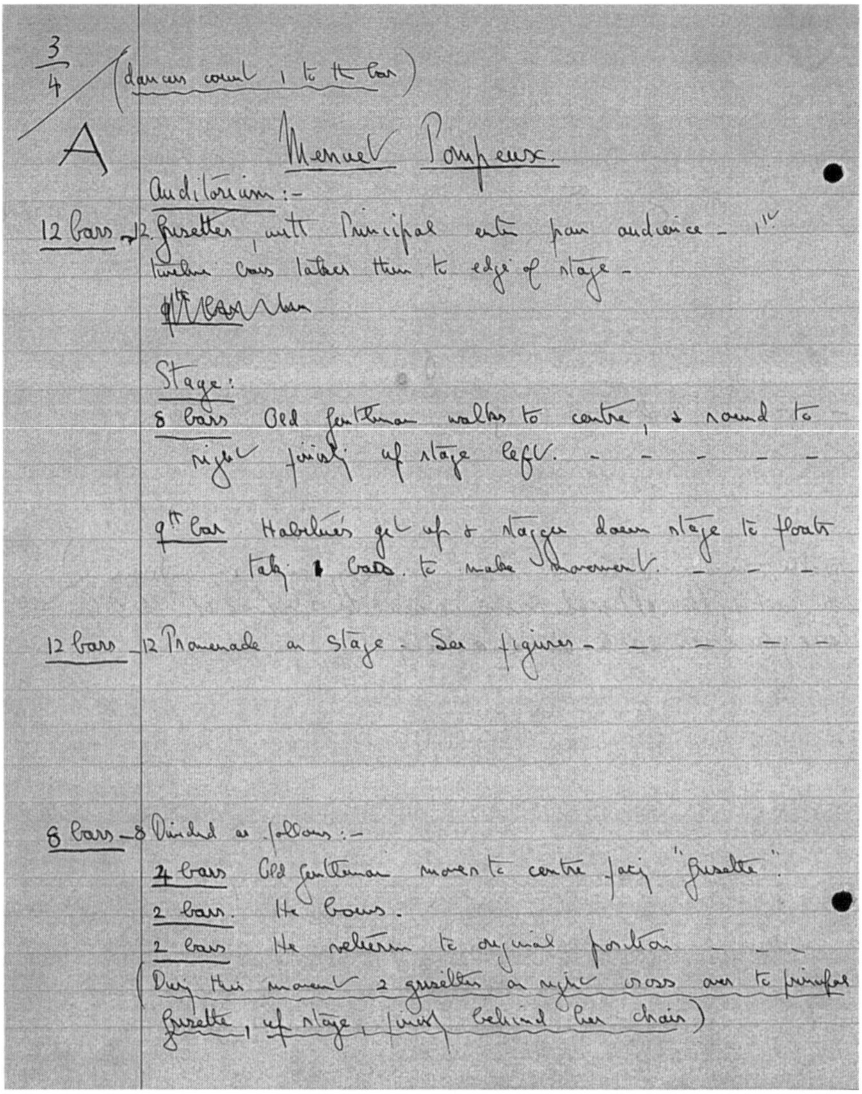

[pp. 21–22]

3/4   (<u>dancers count 1 to the bar</u>)

A   <u>Menuet Pompeux</u>

<u>Auditorium:</u>

<u>12 bars</u> – 12   Grisettes, with principal [grisette], enter from audience. 1st twelve bars
                   takes them to edge of stage.
                   <u>Stage:</u>
                   <u>8 bars</u>. Old gentleman walks to centre, & round to right, finishing upstage
                   left. [DIAGRAM]
                   <u>9th bar</u>. Habitués get up & stagger downstage to floats taking 4 counts to
                   make movement. [DIAGRAM]

<u>12 bars</u> – 12   Promenade on stage. See figures. [DIAGRAMS] (A, B, & C are executed
                   simultaneously.)

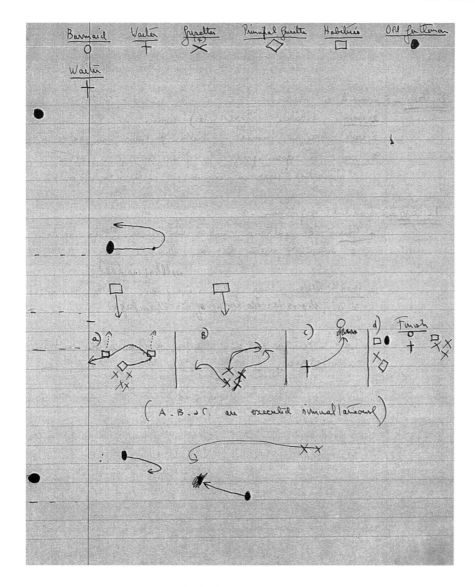

8 bars   − 8   Divided as follows:
<u>4 bars</u>. Old gentleman moves to centre facing grisette.
<u>2 bars</u>. He bows.
<u>2 bars</u>. He returns to original position.
(<u>During this movement 2 grisettes on right cross over
to principal grisette, upstage, finishing behind her
chair</u>.) [DIAGRAMS]

[pp. 23–24]

<u>8 bars</u>   – 8   Divided as follows:
    <u>2 bars</u>. Habitué (<u>right side</u>) rises. [DIAGRAM]
    <u>2 bars</u>. Staggers toward grisette & bows, raising hat.
    <u>2 bars</u>. He goes upstage to chair left side; other habitué rises & crosses to chair right side.

<u>12 bars</u> – 12   Divided as follows:
    <u>4 bars</u>. Old gentleman walks into centre. Claps hands & demands waiter to bring drinks. [DIAGRAM]
    <u>4 bars</u>. Waiter moves round stage *wobbling his head* with bottle towards table, *shows her the brand of his champagne.* [DIAGRAM]
    <u>4 bars</u>. Grisettes get into position for dance. Old gentleman moves back. [DIAGRAM]

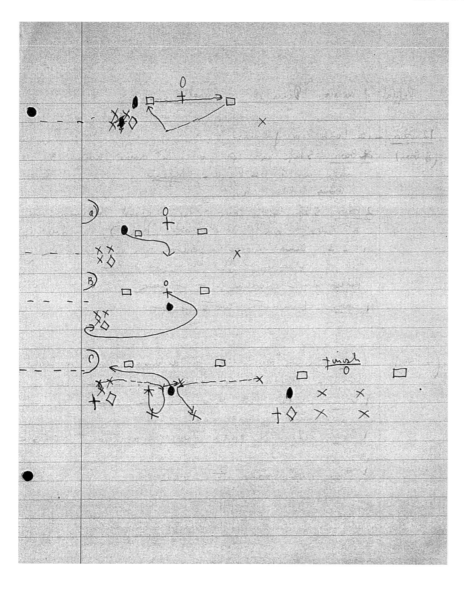

[pp. 25–26]

Repeat of music. Dance of 4 grisettes.

12 bars – 12   Divided as follows:
(8 bars)   2 bars. Step with left foot, 4th croisé (front), 3 steps in 1st, r[ight] – l[eft] – r[ight]. Repeat. Arms Holding skirt.
2 bars. Step left, carry r[ight] leg in grand battement from 4th croisé (front) to effacé (front). Put down in 1st. Arms in 2nd position. Run into middle at end of repeating whole movement for 4 bars. [DIAGRAM]
Repeat whole movement for 4 bars.
1 bar. Run into centre.

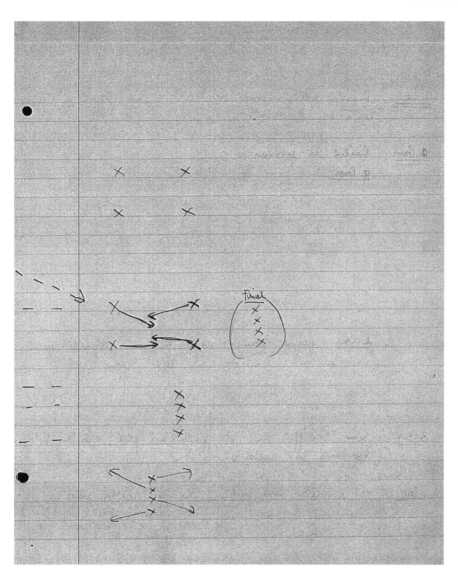

(4 bars)   1 bar. Slow "développés" of alternate legs in second position preceded by little jeté.
1 bar. Repeat with other leg.
1 bar. Repeat in quick succession alternating 3 times.
1 bar. Run back to square. [DIAGRAM]

[pp. 27–28]

<u>4 bars</u>	Repeat same movement as last 4 bars. Running into centre on 1st beat.
<u>10 bars</u>	Divided as follows: <u>8 bars</u> 2 bars. Quick coupés with half-turn towards centre stage—and diagonally into centre—same step. [DIAGRAMS]
<u>3 bars</u>	Slow développé in 4th front on plié. Grisettes holding arms in circle. [DIAGRAM]
<u>1 bar</u>	(Rest.) Grisettes hold position. Principal grisette rises. [DIAGRAM]

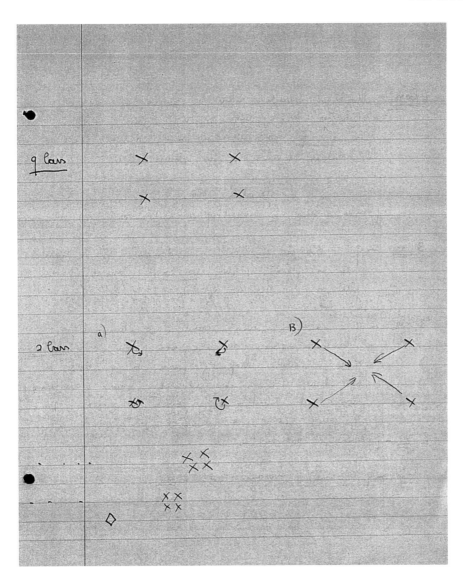

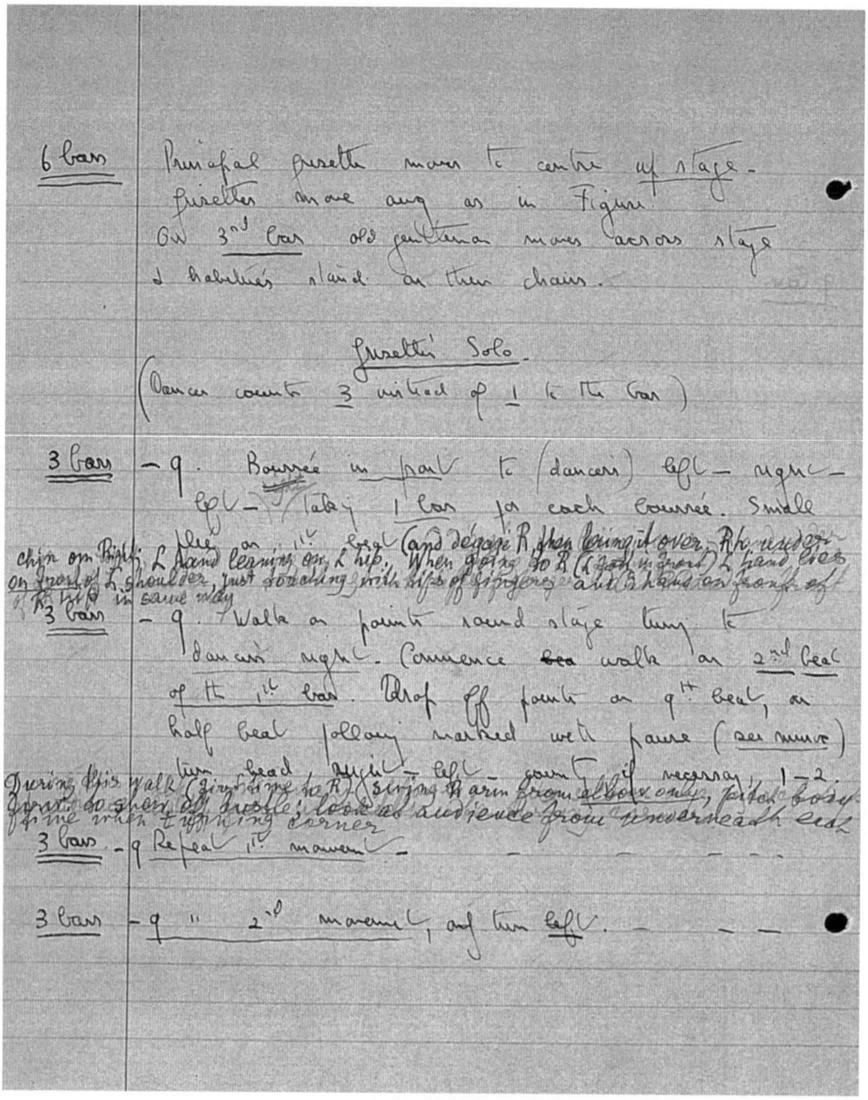

[pp. 29–30]

<u>6 bars</u>	Principal grisette moves to centre <u>upstage</u>. Grisettes move away as in figure. [DIAGRAMS]
	On <u>3rd bar</u> old gentleman moves across stage & habitués stand on their chairs.

<u>Grisette's Solo</u>

(Dancer counts <u>3</u> instead of <u>1</u> to the bar.)

<u>3 bars</u>	– 9	Bourrée <u>in front</u> to (dancer's) left–right–left, taking <u>1 bar</u> for each bourrée. Small plié on 1st beat *(and dégagé R[ight], then bring it over, R[ight] h[and] under chin on Right; L[eft] hand leaning on L[eft] hip. When going to R[ight] (L[eft] foot in front) L[eft] hand lies <u>on front</u> of L[eft] shoulder, just touching with tips of fingers and R[ight] hand on front of R[ight] hip in same way.)* [DIAGRAM]

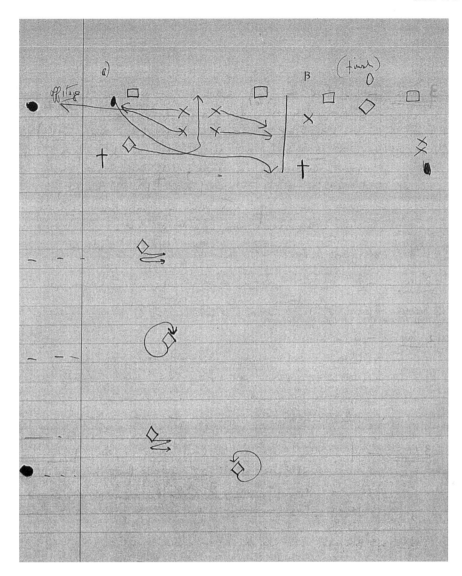

3 bars	– 9	Walk on pointe round stage turning to <u>dancer's right</u>. Commence walk on <u>2nd beat of the 1st bar</u>. Drop off pointe on 9th beat. On half-beat following, marked with pause (<u>see music</u>), turn head, right–left, counting, if necessary 1–2. *During this walk (first time to R[ight]) swinging R[ight] arm from <u>elbow only</u>, pitch body front to to show off bustle; look at audience from underneath each time when turning corner.* [DIAGRAM]
3 bars	– 9	<u>Repeat first movement</u>. [DIAGRAM]
3 bars	– 9	<u>Repeat 2nd movement</u>, only turn <u>left</u>. [DIAGRAM]

[pp. 31–32]

3 bars — 9 Five grands battements in front on pointe moving diagonally downstage.
(The posé is taken *L[eft]–R[ight]–L[eft]–R[ight]–L[eft]* on the <u>beat</u>, and
battement on the <u>half-beat.</u>) On <u>6</u> step on right leg in 4th front, plié
arabesque à terre; [on] <u>7 [and] 8</u> draw back to backbend, leaving front
foot pointed, knee bent. [On] <u>9</u> straighten; [on] half-beat, 2 little steps,
left-right, with hands on hips *and 2 head movements.*
This movement is done towards waiter. DIAGRAM.
*Waiter faints face to wall with hands up flat on it when she shows him her
dessous and gauges the effect on him.*

3 bars — 9 <u>Repeat whole movement diagonally downstage to left towards old
gentleman.</u> [DIAGRAM]
*He crosses himself behind his top hat (with which he shields himself from
the view of her "undies").*

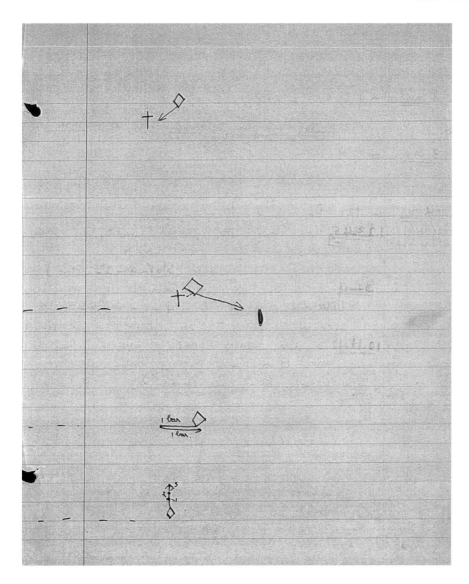

2 bars	– 6	Divide: 1 bar. Walk sideways, left foot–right, left– right, corkscrew right foot with half-turn towards audience closing foot in 1st. 1 bar. <u>Repeat other way.</u> [DIAGRAM]
3 bars	– 9	Step back on r[ight] pointe, close 1st, <u>1st beat</u>. Demi-plié in 1st, <u>2nd beat</u>. Point with finger r[ight] and l[eft], <u>3rd beat</u>. *Points with R[ight] finger to R[ight] and L[eft] calculating for whom better to go.* <u>Repeat this movement for 2 more bars moving back.</u> [DIAGRAM]
1 bar	– 3	"Bourrée en arrière" to centre stage.

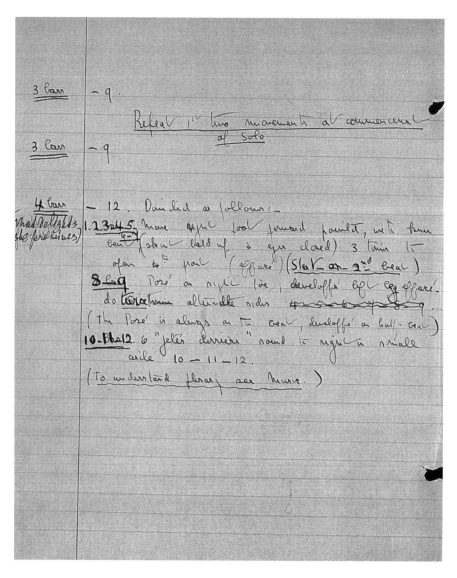

[pp. 33–34]

3 bars – 9   [DIAGRAMS]
Repeat 1st two movements at commencement of solo.

3 bars – 9
4 bars – 12   Divided as follows:
1–2–3–4–5–6–7. Move right foot forward pointed, with knee bent (skirt held up & eyes closed) 3 times to open 4th front (effacé). (Start on 2nd beat.) (*What delights she promises.*) [DIAGRAM]
8–9. Posé on right toe, développé left, leg effacé. Do twice [on] alternate sides. (The posé is always on the beat, développé on half-beat.) [DIAGRAM]
10–11–12. 6 "jetés derrière" round to right in small circle. [DIAGRAM] (To understand phrasing see music.)

1)   ◇   2)

4 beats   ◇ in place

2 beats   ♦

1 bar.

"*Will Be Valuable Someday*":
Preface

1. See, for example, *The Sketch*, 23 May 1934, and 6 Dec. 1939. Three of William Chappell's design sketches were reproduced in London *Vogue* on 30 May 1934.

"*Wonder Child*" *in the School of Hard Knocks:*
De Valois's Early Years

1. Ninette de Valois, *Come Dance With Me: A Memoir, 1898–1956* (London: Dance Books, 1973) p. 33. The book was first published in 1957.
2. For information about de Valois's early life and career, see *Come Dance With Me*, chap. 1; Kathrine Sorley Walker, *Ninette de Valois: Idealist without Illusions* (London: Hamish Hamilton, 1987), chap. 1; "Profile—Ninette de Valois," in *The Ballet Annual* (London: Adam and Charles Black 1948), pp. 54–58. The present discussion also draws on material from my own interviews with Dame Ninette in Barnes on 5 December 1981 and 6 April 1985.
3. *Come Dance With Me*, pp. 10, 5.
4. *Ibid.*, p. 4. "The original house," she wrote, "was burnt in the rising of 1798; the house was now a long two-storied building with a spacious network of basement rooms. It was a typical Irish country house of about 1820–30, late Georgian in part, consisting of one main wing and two smaller ones" (*ibid.*).
5. *Ibid.*, p. 7.
6. *Ibid.*, pp. 17–18.
7. *Ibid.*, pp. 25, 28, 29.
8. Letter to Selma Odom, Nov. 1983.
9. *Come Dance With Me*, pp. 29, 30.
10. *Ibid.*, p. 32.
11. *Ibid.*, p. 31.
12. *Ibid.*, pp. 31–32.
13. "The Teacher of the Russians and News from the Classes," *The Dancing Times*, Aug. 1914, p. 677. Although unsigned, the "News from the Classes" column was written by Richardson.
14. See Beth Genné, "Openly English: Phyllis Bedells and the Birth of British Ballet," *Dance Chronicle*, 18, no. 3 (1995), pp. 437–451.
15. *Come Dance With Me*, p. 36.
16. P.J.S. Richardson, "Dancing in the Christmas Plays," *The Dancing Times*, Jan. 1917, pp. 139–140.
17. *Come Dance With Me*, p. 35. In her description of Madame Rosa, de Valois offers a poignant glimpse into the impoverished old age of nineteenth-century dancers, who counted themselves lucky to secure work as ballet mistress-

es. "She was very poor and lived all alone in a tiny flat in Long Acre; this was as near as she could get to the theatre world, and that world she had served from the age of five. In her room was a delicate painting of herself when young; it showed a petite, frail little person dominated by the nose and a pair of large piercing black eyes. On the last night of the pantomime she would grace the stage in an astounding Edwardian creation, an extremely low cut satin evening dress adorned with clumsy jewels. These jewels, she assured me, were gifts from the young bloods that frequented the Alhambra in her youth. It was known that every bracelet, necklace and brooch spent most of the year in pawn, but all were retrieved for this one spectacular appearance with their owner. She treated her "ladies" as she called the corps de ballet—milling around in monotonous choreographic patterns—with great dignity, discipline, and frigid politeness" (*ibid.*, pp. 35–36).

18. Ninette de Valois, *Step by Step: The Formation of an Establishment* (London: W.H. Allen, 1977), p. 12.
19. *Ibid.*
20. For more information about the standardization movement, see Beth Genné, "P. J. S. Richardson and the Birth of British Ballet" in *Proceedings of the Dance History Scholars Conference*, 1982, pp. 94–101. For the founding of the Association of Operatic Dancing, see Genné, "Openly English," pp. 445–446.
21. See, for example, her demonstration of développés à la seconde, arabesque ouverte, and port de bras in the December 1915 issue (pp. 95–98) and correct and incorrect relevés in the December 1916 issue (p. 82).
22. For a list of her appearances in the late 1910s and early 1920s, see Sorley Walker, *Ninette de Valois*, app. 1, pp. 331–333.
23. *Come Dance With Me*, p. 51.
24. *Ibid.*, p. 52.
25. Quoted in Sorley Walker, *Ninette de Valois*, p. 25. Margaret Craske, at the age of ninety, recalled the experience as "divine." "That was absolutely the most wonderful audience in the world. If they didn't like you they threw things" (quoted *ibid.*).
26. *Come Dance With Me*, p. 49.
27. *Step by Step*, p. 18.
28. *Come Dance With Me*, pp. 45–46.
29. *Ibid.*, p. 46.
30. *Ibid.*, p. 45.
31. *Ibid.*, pp. 46–47.
32. *Step by Step*, pp. 18–19.
33. *Come Dance With Me*, p. 48.
34. *Step by Step*, pp. 20–21.
35. For a fuller discussion of this issue see Genné, "Openly English," pp. 442–444.
36. "All About the Sadler's Wells Ballet," *The Dancing Times*, Mar. 1932, p. 662.
37. Interview with de Valois, 6 Apr. 1985.

"Everything of Value":
De Valois and Diaghilev

1. Ninette de Valois, *Invitation to the Ballet* (London: John Lane, 1937), p. 58.
2. *Ibid.*, p. 14.
3. *Ibid.*, p. 58. For a list of her appearances with the Ballets Russes, see Sorley Walker, *Ninette de Valois*, app. 1, pp. 333–335. Among the roles she played were the Nurse in Nijinska's *Romeo and Juliet*, the Hostess in her *Les Biches*, and Felicia in Massine's *Good-Humoured Ladies*.
4. *Come Dance With Me*, p. 53.
5. *Ibid.*
6. *Invitation to the Ballet*, p. 33.
7. *Ibid.*, p. 34.
8. *Step by Step*, p. 124.
9. In 1924, de Valois studied briefly with Olga Preobrajenska, who was then teaching in Paris. "Help was her aim," she wrote in *Step by Step*, "and in the speediest possible time. I well remember her acute power of observation. During my first few lessons she noted certain weaknesses in my left leg that I always went to great lengths to hide. She…said, 'I will help you here'. She did….They were great technical lessons. At the end of my first series of them we went on a tour of Germany. I felt a different dancer on the stage, and I know that during the tour I danced better than I had ever danced before and, for that matter, afterwards. Her lessons represented the last act of my Russian saga, and seemed to bring my technique to its final point" (pp. 23–24).
10. *Ibid.*, pp. 22–23.
11. *Ibid.*, pp. 21–22.
12. Quoted in Sorley Walker, *Ninette de Valois*, p. 55.
13. Interview with de Valois, 5 Dec. 1981. In *Step by Step* de Valois suggests that it was Diaghilev himself who singled her out during one of the ballet's early rehearsals: "One morning he suddenly appeared flanked by [Francis] Poulenc and [Boris] Kochno at a very embryo *Les Biches corps de ballet* rehearsal. I was quick to note the reason, for Poulenc was convinced, and had told me so, that I was the best little 'Biche' of all the little 'Biches'. I felt myself being singled out, no doubt as the New English Girl. The efforts of my two fans [Poulenc and Kochno] seemed to be falling—as far as I could note out of the corner of an anxious eye—on deaf ears, a misty eyeglass, and a deadly bored face…but suddenly we had arrived at my favourite sequence. The great head nodded, the big mouth grinned, and he tottered out (or so it seemed) followed by the triumphant entourage. Sequel: Nijinska choreographed her role of the Hostess on me" (p. 173).
14. Quoted in Sorley Walker, *Ninette de Valois*, p. 149.
15. *Invitation to the Ballet*, p. 69.
16. *Ibid.*, p. 57.
17. *Come Dance With Me*, pp. 67–68.
18. *Ibid.*, p. 68.
19. Quoted in Sorley Walker, *Ninette de Valois*, p. 149.
20. Tamara Karsavina, "The Influence of Diaghileff on Ballet in England," *The Dancing Times*, Oct. 1935, p. 13.
21. Quoted in Sorley Walker, *Ninette de Valois*, p. 53.

22. Ninette de Valois, "Modern Choregraphy," *The Dancing Times*, pt. 5, May 1933, p. 123.

23. *Come Dance With Me*, p. 33.

24. "Modern Choregraphy," pt. 5, p. 122.

25. *Step by Step*, pp. 188–189.

26. *Ibid.*, pp. 176–177. It is possible that the publication in 1930 of Tamara Karsavina's *Theatre Street*, with its affectionate reminiscence of her school-days at the Imperial Ballet School, reinforced de Valois's commitment to a company-affiliated school and helped popularize the idea. The book was solicited and edited by Arnold Haskell, whom de Valois chose to head the Sadler's Wells school in 1947.

27. Act II of *Swan Lake* was mounted in 1932, and the two acts of *Coppélia* in 1933. *The Nutcracker*, *Giselle*, and the full-length *Swan Lake* entered the repertory in 1934.

28. For a list of the company's productions from 1928 to 1955, see Mary Clarke, *The Sadler's Wells Ballet: A History and An Appreciation* (London: Adam and Charles Black, 1955), app. E, pp. 321–337.

29. Ninette de Valois, "The Future of the Ballet," *The Dancing Times*, Feb. 1926, pp. 589–591.

30. Ninette de Valois, "The Sadler's Wells Organisation," *The Dancing Times*, Aug. 1952, p. 656.

31. In one of my interviews with her (5 Dec. 1981), de Valois told me that she did not see the productions of *Swan Lake* and *Giselle* presented by the Diaghilev company at the Royal Opera House, Covent Garden, in 1911, or the *Giselle* danced by the Pavlova company at Oscar Hammerstein's London Opera House two years later.

32. *Come Dance With Me*, p. 48.

33. *Step by Step*, p. 126.

34. *Come Dance With Me*, p. 66. In *Invitation to the Ballet* de Valois noted that the ballet was revived by Anatole Wilzak and his wife, Ludmila Schollar. There was "an additional number for the swans arranged by Nijinska and placed in the second act just before the Swan Princess's solo," and "the first act *pas de trois* was introduced into the third act in lieu of the dance of the fiancées" (p. 43). Of Trefilova she wrote: "The stature of this particular ballerina and the poise of her head place her in a class apart. She is the most perfect study in proportions I have ever seen, and this remarkable physical symmetry always found its complement in her work. Many of the greatest ballerinas have fortunate and unfortunate distinctions or mannerisms. Trefilova, in her performance, seems to possess no such individual traits, and this constitutes her rarity. She was, as the Swan Princess, a perfect classical and academic study, to be likened in detail and finish to a drawing by Ingres; and, to complete this unusual portrait, an actress of great qualities" (*ibid.*, p. 44).

35. Among the snippets presented in London in the 1920s were the "Doll Dance" from Act II mounted by Nicolas Legat in 1925 and an unspecified excerpt presented by the Association of Operatic Dancing in 1929 ("The Sitter Out," *The Dancing Times*, Feb. 1925, p. 511; "Operatic Dancing: Display at the Gaiety Theatre," The Times, 5 July 1929, p. 14).

36. *Come Dance With Me*, pp. 110–111.

37. *Step by Step*, p. 29.

38. For a discussion of these scores, now in the collection of the Harvard Theatre Museum, see Roland John Wiley, *Tchaikovsky's Ballets: "Swan Lake," "Sleeping Beauty," "Nutcracker"* (Oxford: Oxford University Press, 1985).

39. *Invitation to the Ballet*, pp. 244–245.

40. *Step by Step*, p. 124. Here, de Valois not only describes the Nijinska version but also claims that Diaghilev "always preferred" it to the original. After she left the company, he asked her "to teach the more modern arrangement to Madame Legat."

41. *Come Dance With Me*, p. 112.

42. *Step by Step*, p. 125.

43. In *Step by Step*, de Valois noted other choreographic changes introduced by Diaghilev: "I have distinct memories at the Alhambra of at least two of the ballerinas executing fouettés in the wood scene, to the exclusion of some of Petipa's choreography. Sergueeff most certainly never included them in any part of this scene in his production for us at Sadler's Wells. 'Florestan and His Two Sisters' also had many innovations introduced by Nijinska; these were the arrangements that I executed later with Nikitina and Lifar, in the condensed one-act version of…*Aurora's Wedding*. Further innovations of this same *pas de trois* took place later in the Diaghilev Company by Balanchine" (p. 125).

44. Interview with de Valois, 5 Dec. 1981.

45. *Step by Step*, p. 174.

46. "What Diaghileff Has Taught Us," *The Dancing Times*, Dec. 1919, pp. 176–177.

47. Ninette de Valois, "Modern Choreography," pt. 4, *The Dancing Times*, Apr. 1933, p. 10.

48. Clarke, *The Sadler's Wells Ballet*, p. 37.

49. Interview with de Valois, 6 Apr. 1985.

50. *Step by Step*, pp. 87–88.

51. Interview with de Valois, 5 Dec. 1981.

52. *Come Dance With Me*, p. 112.

53. *Ibid.*, p. 114.

54. Alicia Markova, *Markova Remembers* (Boston: Little, Brown, 1986), p. 44.

55. P.W. Manchester, *Vic-Wells: A Ballet Progress* (London: Gollancz, 1943), p. 25.

56. "All About the Sadler's Wells Ballet," *The Dancing Times*, Mar. 1932, p. 662.

57. *Come Dance With Me*, p. 68.

58. Quoted in Sorley Walker, *Ninette de Valois*, p. 55. De Valois told me the same story during my interview with her in April 1985.

"The Future of Ballet":
De Valois and Modern Choreography

1. Interview with de Valois, 5 Dec. 1981.

2. Quoted in Anna Blewchamp, "Gweneth Lloyd and *The Wise Virgins*: The Development of an Artist, the Reconstruction of the Ballet" (M.F.A. thesis, York University, 1992), p. 29.

3. Lilly Grove, *Dancing* (London: Longmans, Green, 1895), pp. 384–385. This is from Chapter 8, "The Practical Use of Dancing from Notes by Mrs.

Wordsworth."

4. *Come Dance With Me*, p. 29.

5. *Ibid.*, p. 71.

6. Ninette de Valois, "The Future of the Ballet," *The Dancing Times*, Feb. 1926, pp. 589–593. The photograph appears on page 591; the school announcement on page 590. Throughout this period, de Valois used a "mid-Channel" spelling for the word "choreography" and its variants. Hence, the title of her school—the Academy of Choregraphic Art. I am grateful to Ivor Guest for pointing out that the spelling adopted by de Valois was used consistently at this time by P.J.S. Richardson, the editor of *The Dancing Times*, although it is worth noting that de Valois herself added the "o" to the term in *Invitation to the Ballet*, published in 1937. Mary Clarke has said that the title of de Valois's new academy was the suggestion of Cyril W. Beaumont: "In the course of her search for a suitable name for the School, she consulted Cyril Beaumont and explained to him that she wanted the emphasis to be on choreography. He considered and then suggested she should call it 'the Academy of Choregraphic Art'" (Clarke, *The Sadler's Wells Ballet*, p. 37).

7. *Ibid.*, p. 589.

8. *Ibid.*, p. 593.

9. *Ibid.*, p. 589.

10. *Ibid.*

11. *Ibid.*, pp. 589, 591.

12. De Valois was not alone in this belief. In 1924, two years before her article was published, the Ginner-Mawer School had added Cecchetti classes to its "revised Greek" curriculum. The sharp split between modern dance and ballet characteristic of the United States in the 1930s had no parallel in England in the 1920s.

13. "The Future of the Ballet," p. 589.

14. *Ibid.*, pp. 591, 593.

15. *Ibid.*, p. 593.

16. *Ibid.*, p. 589.

17. Norman Marshall, *The Other Theatre* (London: John Lehmann, 1947), p. 15.

18. For the effect of market economics on the early development of the Ballets Russes, see Lynn Garafola, *Diaghilev's Ballets Russes* (New York: Oxford University Press, 1989), pp. 177–200.

19. Marshall, *The Other Theatre*, pp. 140–141.

20. *Ibid.*, p. 54.

21. *Ibid.*, pp. 54–55.

22. Terence Gray, *Dance-Drama: Experiments in the Art of the Theatre* (Cambridge: W. Heffer, 1926), p. 25.

23. *Ibid.*, p. 24.

24. *Ibid.*, p. 25.

25. For the text of *The Scorpions of Ysit*, see *ibid.*, pp. 114–123.

26. *Ibid.*, p. 27.

27. For Gray's view of Fokine and the "Russian Ballet," see *ibid.*, pp. 28–30 and 32–34; for the influence of the Moscow Art Theater on Fokine, see Garafola, *Diaghilev's Ballets Russes*, pp. 19–24.

28. *Come Dance With Me*, p. 87.

29. Marshall, *The Other Theatre*, pp. 62–63.

30. *Ibid.*, p. 140.
31. For the origin and various manifestations of the movement, see Victor H. Miesel's introduction to *Voices of German Expressionism* (Englewood Cliffs, N.J.: Prentice-Hall, 1970), pp. 1–12.
32. "A Chronology of the Ballet in England 1910–1935," *The Dancing Times*, Oct. 1935, p. 8.
33. *Invitation to the Ballet*, p. 178.
34. Quoted in Sorley Walker, *Ninette de Valois*, p. 77.
35. *Ibid.*
36. "The Sitter Out," *The Dancing Times*, Feb. 1928, p. 51.
37. Quoted in David Vaughan, *Frederick Ashton and His Ballets* (New York: Knopf, 1977), p. 51.
38. *Ibid.*
39. "The Sitter Out," *The Dancing Times*, Mar. 1927, p. 716.
40. "The Sitter Out," *The Dancing Times*, Feb. 1928, p. 671.
41. *Ibid.*, pp. 672–674.
42. Over the years her views have changed. Now, she views the adoption of modern dance techniques in ballet with considerable alarm and sees the Graham-based "school"—in England, at least—as having a strong anticlassical bias.
43. Quoted in Sorley Walker, *Ninette de Valois*, p. 85.
44. *Come Dance With Me*, p. 88.

"A Strange, Noble, Unforgettable Figure": De Valois, Yeats, Butler, and Rambert

1. Quoted in Sorley Walker, *Ninette de Valois*, p. 96.
2. *Step by Step*, pp. 181–182. De Valois also notes cannily that Yeats was concerned about the fact that the Gate Theatre, a repertory theater, was about to open in Dublin, and feared the effect of its competition with the Abbey.
3. *Ibid.*, p. 180.
4. See Sorley Walker, *Ninette de Valois*, pp. 93–96 (*Fighting the Waves*), 118–119 (*The Dreaming of the Bones*), and 144–146 (*The King of the Great Clock Tower*).
5. W.B. Yeats, *Collected Plays*, 2nd ed. (London: Macmillan, 1952), p. 632. In her book *Gendering Bodies/Performing Art: Dance and Literature in Early Twentieth-Century British Culture* (Ann Arbor: University of Michigan Press, 1995), Amy Koritz devotes an entire chapter to the early Plays for Dancers, but fails to mention that Yeats revived or adapted them for de Valois. Although they were conceived for and initially performed by Michio Ito, a man, Yeats seems to have had no problem in reviving them for de Valois, a woman, or in envisioning her in roles conceived for a man. Given the emphasis on gender in Koritz's book, this oversight is problematic. Additionally, in a study purporting to show how by the late 1920s "ballet...defined what constituted dance as an art form for British culture" (p. 10) it is odd that neither de Valois nor any of her writings is mentioned.
6. Ninette de Valois, *The Cycle and Other Poems* (London: Sadler's Wells Trust, 1985).
7. *Step by Step*, pp. 183–184.
8. *Ibid.*, p. 180.

9. *Ibid.*, p. 183.

10. William P. Malm, *Japanese Music and Musical Instruments* (Rutland, Vt./Tokyo: Charles E. Tuttle Co., 1959), p. 119. I would like to thank both Professor Malm and Joyce Rutherford Malm for sharing their deep knowledge of Japanese music and dance with me.

11. Quoted in Sorley Walker, *Ninette de Valois*, p. 96.

12. *Step by Step*, p. 184.

13. For biographical information about Lilian Baylis (1874–1937), see Richard Findlater, *Lilian Baylis: The Lady of the Old Vic* (London: Allen Lane, 1975).

14. Although Baylis is not discussed in the book, she was certainly part of the milieu described in Martha Vicinus's pioneering study *Independent Women: Work and Community for Single Women 1850–1920* (Chicago: University of Chicago Press, 1985), especially chapter 6 ("A Community Ideal for the Poor").

15. *Step by Step*, p. 35.

16. *Ibid.*, p. 32.

17. *Invitation to the Ballet*, p. 86.

18. *Ibid.*, p. 87.

19. *Ibid.*, p. 86.

20. *Ibid.*, p. 106.

21. *Ibid.*, p. 86.

22. Mary Clarke tells the story of how in the course of rehearsals for *The Nutcracker*, "Sergueeff one day noticed Elsa Lanchester, then a member of the Old Vic Shakespeare Company, rehearsing for Ariel in *The Tempest*. He liked the way she moved and decided she would do a better Danse Arabe in *Casse Noisette* than any of the dancers. He rushed upstairs to the office, where he cried excitedly, 'Dramateek lady! dramateek lady!' and gesticulated wildly. When the management realised what he was getting at they quailed from the task of explaining to Sergueeff that Elsa Lanchester belonged to the drama and not the ballet company, and instead asked her what she thought about the suggestion. She gladly agreed to perform the Danse Arabe" (Clarke, *The Sadler's Wells Ballet*, pp. 94–95).

23. Marie Rambert, *Quicksilver: An Autobiography* (London: Macmillan, 1972), p. 157.

24. Interview with de Valois, 6 Apr. 1985.

25. *Come Dance With Me*, pp. 151–152.

26. I am grateful to Jane Pritchard and Selma Odom for the 1909 date, which is based on new material indicating that Rambert entered the Dalcroze institute in Geneva a year earlier than previously thought.

27. This story was recounted to me by Jane Pritchard, who attended the memorial service.

28. De Valois to Rambert, 12 July 1937, Rambert Dance Company Archives.

29. John Gruen, transcript of interview with Marie Rambert, 30 July 1974, p. 43. Oral History Archive, Dance Collection, New York Public Library.

30. *Ibid.*, p. 55.

31. *Ibid.*, p. 62.

32. Interview with William Chappell, London, 4 Apr. 1985.

33. Interview with de Valois, 5 Dec. 1981.

34. Rambert, *Quicksilver*, p. 123.

35. De Valois told me the story in December 1981 and repeated it in the television documentary, *Frederick Ashton: A Real Choreographer* (BBC-TV, in association with R.M. Productions, Munich, 1979).

36. *Step by Step*, p. 44.

37. *Ibid.*, p. 45.

38. *Ibid.*, pp. 45–46.

39. *Invitation to the Ballet*, p. 149.

40. Mary Clarke, *Dancers of Mercury: The Story of Ballet Rambert* (London: Adam and Charles Black, 1962), pp. 75–76.

41. Quoted *ibid.*, p. 76.

42. Agnes de Mille, *Dance to the Piper* (Boston: Little, Brown, 1951), p. 142.

43. Quoted in Judith Chazin-Bennahum, *The Ballets of Antony Tudor: Studies in Psyche and Satire* (New York: Oxford University Press, 1994), p. 25.

44. Quoted in Zoe Dominic and John Selwyn Gilbert, *Frederick Ashton: A Choreographer and His Ballets* (Chicago: Henry Regnery Company, 1973), p. 38.

45. Quoted *ibid.*, pp. 76–77.

46. Interview with de Valois, 6 Apr. 1985.

47. De Valois, "The Future of the Ballet," p. 593.

48. For a complete list of her ballets, see Sorley Walker, *Ninette de Valois*, app. 2, pp. 341–352.

49. Although de Valois makes no mention of Borlin's version of the ballet, she does offer a brief tribute to him in *Invitation to the Ballet*. "This young artist," she wrote, "showed some promise as a choreographer; in fact *El Greco* and *Les Vierges Folles* were two works that in their own line were utterly satisfactory, the former having a nobility and simplicity about it that struck an unusual and courageous note at that time. One can further recall *Dansgille* and *Nuit de Saint-Jean*, two ballets which made full use of the Swedish folk dance and music to some real advantage" (p. 180). Given the Ballets Russes touring schedule, it is unlikely that de Valois saw Borlin's production of *La Création du Monde*.

50. Sorley Walker, *Ninette de Valois*, p. 107.

51. Quoted in Nesta Macdonald, *Diaghilev Observed by Critics in England and the United States 1911–1929* (New York: Dance Horizons, 1975), p. 353.

52. Interview with de Valois, 5 Dec. 1981.

53. Cyril W. Beaumont, *Complete Book of Ballets* (London: Putnam, 1937), p. 932.

54. De Valois, "Modern Choreography," pt. 3, *The Dancing Times*, Mar. 1933, pp. 669–670.

Bar aux Folies-Bergère

1. Marie Rambert, *Quicksilver: An Autobiography* (London: Macmillan, 1972), p. 157.

2. For an account of his multifaceted career, see Ashley Dukes, *The Scene is Changed* (London: Macmillan, 1942).

3. Interview with Angus Morrison, London, 7 Apr. 1985. For Samuel Courtauld and his collection, see John House *et al.*, *Impressionism for England: Samuel Courtauld as Patron and Collector* (London: Courtauld Institute Galleries, 1994).

4. Clarke, *Dancers of Mercury*, p. 94.

5. Interview with de Valois, 6 Apr. 1985.

6. *Ibid.*

7. *Ibid.*

8. Ninette de Valois, "Modern Choregraphy," *The Dancing Times*, pt. 1 ("Introductory"), Jan. 1933, pp. 434–436; pt. 2, Feb. 1933, pp. 549–552; pt. 3 ("Production: Theatrical Representation"), Mar. 1933, pp. 668–670; pt. 4 ("Décor and Costume"), Apr. 1933, pp. 9–10; pt. 5 ("The Classical Dancer of To-day"), May 1933, pp. 122–125. Throughout the series, de Valois retains the Gallicized spelling of the word "choregraphy" (and its variants) that appears in her 1926 article, "The Future of the Ballet," and in the name of her school.

9. "Modern Choregraphy," pt. 3, p. 668.

10. *Step by Step*, p. 56.

11. The pieces were "Danse Villageoise," "Mélancolie," "Tourbillon," "Mauresque," "Idylle," "Menuet pompeux," and "Scherzo-valse."

12. Constant Lambert, *Music Ho! A Study of Music in Decline*, 3rd ed., introd. Arthur Hutchings (London: Faber and Faber, 1966), pp. 171–172.

13. Rollo H. Myers, *Chabrier and his Circle* (London: Dent, 1969, pp. 5–6, 148–154. The portraits of Chabrier are reproduced in Denis Rouart and Daniel Wildenstein, *Edouard Manet: Catalogue raisonné* (Lausanne: Bibliothèque des Arts, 1975), 1, no. 364, and 2, no. 29.

14. Lambert, *Music Ho!*, pp. 172–173.

15. For stage photographs showing the backdrop and for excerpts from reviews discussing the use of El Greco's work in the production, see Bengt Hager, *Ballets Suédois (The Swedish Ballet)*, trans. Ruth Sharman (New York: Abrams, 1990), pp. 105–109.

16. "Modern Choregraphy," pt. 2, p. 550.

17. *Ibid.*

18. Interview with de Valois, 6 Apr. 1985.

19. "Modern Choregraphy," pt. 2, p. 550.

20. *Ibid.*

21. Interview with de Valois, 6 Apr. 1985.

22. "Modern Choregraphy," pt. 2, p. 550.

23. *Ibid.*

24. *Ibid.*

25. According to Angus Morrison, the order of the pieces was as follows: "Danse villageoise" (overture), "Mélancolie," "Tourbillon," "Mauresque," "Idylle," "Mauresque," "Menuet pompeux," "Scherzo-valse," "Mélancolie" (reprise). I am grateful to him for this information as well for discussing Lambert's editorial changes with me.

26. "Modern Choregraphy," pt. 2, pp. 551–552.

27. *Ibid.*, pp. 550–551.

28. "Modern Choregraphy," pt. 3, p. 668.

29 *Ibid.*

30. "Modern Choregraphy," pt. 3, p. 670.

31. *Ibid.*

32. *Ibid.*

33. Beaumont, *Complete Book of Ballets*, pp. 937–938.

34. "Modern Choregraphy," pt. 4, p. 10.

35. Interview with William Chappell, London, 4 Apr. 1985. Chappell was not the first artist whom de Valois approached to design the ballet. Another artist had submitted sketches that she found unacceptable.

36. *Ibid.*

37. *Ibid.*

38. *Ibid.*

39. *Ibid.* Such economy was typical of Rambert's productions. In *Frederick Ashton and His Ballets*, David Vaughan describes the "budget" for Ashton's *Capriol Suite*, which Chappell designed in 1930: "The ballet was mounted with the economy that was by now characteristic of Rambert's productions: for the costumes she and Chappell bought beige linen at sixpence a yard and pink linen at two shillings and sixpence a yard at John Barker's basement in Kensington High Street, and he decorated them with black tape.... The total cost of the production was £5" (pp. 36, 38).

40. Interview with Chappell.

41. *Ibid.*

42. "Modern Choregraphy," pt. 4, p. 90.

43. Interview with de Valois, 6 Apr. 1985. Unfortunately, with the exception of Diana Gould Menuhin, no one I have interviewed remembers exactly how the Can-Can dancers were "individualized." Lady Menuhin makes it clear, however, that her character—Grille d'Egout—was meant to be the comedienne of the group, and that she and Markova played off of one another in vying for the attention of the gentlemen at the bar (interview with Lady Menuhin).

44. Interview with Alicia Markova, London, 6 Oct. 1980. See, also, Sorley Walker, *Ninette de Valois*, p. 143.

45. Quoted in Anton Dolin, *Markova: Her Life and Art* (London: W.H. Allen, 1953), p. 145.

46. Beaumont, *Complete Book of Ballets*, p. 938.

47. Interview with de Valois, 6 Apr. 1985. This is corroborated by Gould, who told me that she was eager to use her talents as a comedienne. She recalls too, how well organized and interesting de Valois was in rehearsal. Gould's entrance with Markova down the aisle of the Mercury Theatre, trading looks and flirting with the men in the audience, established their characters even before they reached the stage.

48. D.D., "A Charming New Ballet: Manet's 'Bar aux Folies-Bergère,'" *The Daily Telegraph*, 16 May 1934.

49. Interview with de Valois, 6 Apr. 1985.

50. Beaumont, *Complete Book of Ballets*, p. 938.

51. "Mercury Theatre: A Season of Ballet," *The Times*, 16 May 1934, p. 14.

52. "The Sitter Out," *The Dancing Times*, June 1934, p. 232.

53. Interview with de Valois, 6 Apr. 1985.

54. For a discussion of the women who tended bar at the Folies-Bergère and the barmaid in Manet's painting, see T.J. Clarke, *The Painting of Modern Life: Paris in the Art of Manet and His Followers* (New York: Knopf, 1985), chap. 4. For other useful background, see Joel Isaacson, "Impressionism and Journalistic Illustration," *Arts Magazine*, June 1982, pp. 95–115.

55. Interview with de Valois, 6 Apr. 1985. This seems at odds with the ending described by Beaumont—"resting her chin on her knucles, [she] stares fixedly into space" (*Complete Book of Ballets*, p. 938).

56. *Ibid.*
57. "The Sitter Out," *The Dancing Times*, June 1934, p. 232.
58. "Mercury Theatre: A Season of Ballet," *The Times*, 16 May 1934, p. 14.
59. D.D., "A Charming New Ballet: Manet's 'Bar aux Folies-Bergère,'" *The Daily Telegraph*, 16 May 1934.
60. "The Sitter Out," *The Dancing Times*, June 1934, p. 232.
61. Interview with de Valois, 6 Apr. 1985.
62. Fernau Hall, *Modern English Ballet* (London: Andrew Melrose, 1950), p. 103.
63. I am grateful to Jane Pritchard for the information about *Pippa Passes*.

The Notebook

1. Interview with Elisabeth Schooling, London, July 1986.
2. Interview with de Valois, 6 Apr. 1985.
3. Interview with Lady Menuhin.
4. Interview with de Valois, 6 Apr. 1985.
5. Interview with Lady Menuhin.
6. *Ibid.*
7. Interview with de Valois, 6 Apr. 1985.
8. Interviews with Lady Menuhin, Elisabeth Schooling, and Sally Gilmour (London, July 1986).
9. During my interview with her in 1985, de Valois insisted that were *Bar* to be revived it had to be mounted as a "chamber ballet" in a venue with the intimacy of the Mercury Theatre. In fact, she was very concerned when Ballet Rambert performed the work in large houses on tour and also when the company allowed the ballet to be televised. "[They] thought you could transfer things from the theater to television without change, but of course you can't." These concerns were the cause of a slight rift, later healed, between her and Ashley Dukes. "He said there was nothing I could do about it: the ballet belonged to them." "In spite of everything," she added, "I personally adored him. I thought he was a marvelous man,...just out of this world,...[and] a wonderful writer."

Index

STUDIES IN DANCE HISTORY is a monographic series published semiannually by the Society of Dance History Scholars on the history of dance and related disciplines. International in outlook, the series is an important forum for research throughout the discipline as well as a source of long out-of-print classics. Lively, informative, and generously illustrated, STUDIES IN DANCE HISTORY offers a body of scholarly writing that no one seriously interested in dance can do without.

Editorial inquiries and submissions: Judith C. Bennahum, Department of Theatre and Dance, Fine Arts Center, University of New Mexico, Albuquerque, NM 87131.

Subscriptions, back issues, changes of address: Marge Maddux, Dance Program, University of Minnesota, 108 Norris Hall, 172 Pillsbury Drive, S.E., Minnepolis, MN 55455; PHONE 612-626-7211; FAX 612-625-2849.

Subscription price is $45/year or $80 for two years. Postage outside North America is an additional $10/year or $20 for two years. The single copy price is $21.95. Postage and handling rates are $3 for the first book and $1 for each additional book in North America; elsewhere, $5 for the first book and $3 for each additional book. All orders must be prepaid in U.S. funds. Checks should be made out to the Society of Dance History Scholars and sent to Marge Maddux, Dance Program, University of Minnesota, 108 Norris Hall, 172 Pillsbury Drive, S.E., Minneapolis, MN 55455.

European distributor: Dance Books Limited, 9 Cecil Court, London WC2N 4EZ, United Kingdom. Single copy price is £12.50 inland and £15 overseas.

STUDIES IN DANCE HISTORY